Jesus Christ after Two Thousand Years

Jesus Christ after Two Thousand Years

The Definitive Interpretation of His Personality

Frank O'Hara

WIPF & STOCK · Eugene, Oregon

JESUS CHRIST AFTER TWO THOUSAND YEARS
The Definitive Interpretation of His Personality

Copyright © 2013 Frank O'Hara. All rights reserved. Except for brief quotations in critical publications or reviews, no part of this book may be reproduced in any manner without prior written permission from the publisher. Write: Permissions, Wipf and Stock Publishers, 199 W. 8th Ave., Suite 3, Eugene, OR 97401.

Wipf & Stock
An Imprint of Wipf and Stock Publishers
199 W. 8th Ave., Suite 3
Eugene, OR 97401

www.wipfandstock.com

ISBN 13: 978-1-62032-610-7

Manufactured in the U.S.A.

For Hilary

Fair in every part, my true love,
no fault in all thy fashioning!

—Song of Songs, 4:7 (Ronald Knox translation)

Contents

Preface   ix

List of Abbreviations   xiii

Introduction   1

1   The Word Was Made Flesh   3

2   The Invisible Becomes Visible   6

3   The Inaudible Becomes Audible   10

4   The Intangible Becomes Tangible   14

5   The Impalpable Becomes Palpable: Atonement   18

6   *Cor Iesu Christi, Cor Verbi Incarnati, quia Cor Verbi Incarnatum*   25

7   Technical Aspects of Translation Christology   36

8   Translations as the Communication of Meaning   39

9   *Finitum Capax Infiniti* (Martin Luther): Man as God's Image   51

10   *Finitum non Capax Infiniti* (John Calvin): Mapping the Infinite on the Finite   56

11   Religious Aspects of Translation Christology   65

12   God Revealed by Jesus Christ: The Eternal Father   66

13   God Revealed in Jesus Christ: The Incarnate Son   76

14   God Revealed Through Jesus Christ: The Holy Spirit   86

15   The Incarnation Realized in Fact: Christogenesis   92

16   The Incarnation Fulfilled in History: The Cosmic Christ   102

Appendix A: A Note on Aristotelian and Scholastic Concepts   105

Appendix B: The Impassibility of God: A Critique   108

Appendix C: The Resurrection of Jesus Christ   118

Appendix D: Toward a Modern Theory of the Holy Trinity   126

Bibliography   133

Preface

THE MAIN BODY OF this work was contained in a PhD thesis which I submitted in November 1971.[1] At that time I was registered as an external student of the University of London. The thesis was supervised by the late Professor E. L. Mascall of King's College London.

However, the theory of incarnation as translation, on which the thesis was based, had been outlined in 1955. I was almost twenty-five years old, and I had recently left the Gregorian University, Rome. Likewise, I had outlined the theories of the Resurrection of Jesus Christ and of the Trinity, contained in Appendix C and D of this book, at the same time. I note my age in relation to these ideas because it was at about the age of twenty-five that Albert Einstein began to develop his theory of special relativity. This was also the age that St. Thomas Aquinas wrote his *De Veritate*, which contained the germ of his philosophical system. I mention this to show that important discoveries can be made by young people.

About the time of my wedding in 1959, I put my theories into a work of some 103 pages. In 1967 I produced twenty-five copies of this work and sent it to some publishers, without success.

After I had completed degrees in mathematics and statistics at the University of London in 1977, I obtained permission from Dr. James Leicester (the Director of Northern Polytechnic, where I was lecturing in statistics) to do my next degree in theology. I sent a copy of my 1967 manuscript to Professor Eric Mascall at King's College, London, and he accepted me as a student for a research degree in theology. Over the next few years I wrote my thesis.

One incident during that time assumed crucial importance for me. Professor Mascall was a very conservative theologian, and I discovered that some of my fundamental views differed from his. In particular, I had decided that the theory of a specially created soul in man (which I had come to call the "neo-Platonic" soul) was not compatible with modern thought. I was not at that time familiar with Charles Darwin's statement

1. See Introduction, note 2.

in *The Descent of Man* (Princeton University Press, 1981, p. 105) that "the difference in mind between man and the higher animals, great as it is, is certainly one of degree and not of kind."

Some way into my discussions with Professor Mascall I had come to feel that our difference on this point was so profound that I might not be able to continue with my thesis. I wrote to him to this effect. He wrote a short reply, on May 27, 1969. The key sentence in that note, in my view, was, "I am not here as a judge of orthodoxy." So I proceeded with the thesis.

In September 1971, before I had actually obtained the PhD, I placed a short article entitled "Incarnation as Translation" with *New Blackfriars*, edited at that time by the late Father Herbert McCabe, OP. However, subsequent attempts to publish the thesis in book form were unsuccessful. Finally, I set aside this project when I moved from polytechnic lecturing into the civil service in May 1973.

On my retirement from the civil service in March 1995, I began to think of trying again to rewrite my thesis for publication. I attended some seminars at my old college, King's College London, and began rewriting in the winter of 1996–1997.

It is usual to acknowledge the help received from other people in producing works such as this. I have already mentioned the late Professor Eric Mascall and the encouragement he gave me even when he disagreed with my opinions. Some will regard this as normal behavior for an academic, but I have not found all academics to be equally tolerant. And so I record my gratitude to Professor Mascall here.

If I were to mention everyone who helped me along the way toward publishing this work, the list would be a long one. I must however mention my philosophy lecturer in Australia, the late Father John Savage, MSC, who taught me from 1948 to 1951 in Croydon, Victoria. A good philosophical foundation is undoubtedly essential to the writing of systematic theology, and John Savage was unanimously regarded as the best philosophy teacher they had ever had at Croydon. Also, among my lecturers at the Gregorian University in Rome I am indebted to the late Father Bernard Lonergan, SJ, who has come to be widely regarded as a seminal thinker for modern transcendental Thomism.

Of course not all of one's influences in creating a work such as this are directly academic. The person who springs to mind here is my headmaster, Father John Doyle, MSC, at Downlands College, Toowoomba. A charismatic man who had a great impact on the students of the college, John Doyle was in 1951 appointed Vicar Apostolic of Port Moresby in Papua New Guinea. He visited the philosophy students at Croydon just before taking up his appointment. I was about to leave for Rome to study theology at the Gregorian University. Nodding toward me, he said to the assembled students, "Could this come from Jandowae?" referring to my hometown in southeast Queensland. This was clearly a veiled reference to the first chapter of St. John's Gospel, where the disciples introduced Nathanael to Jesus and Nathanael said, "Can anything good come from Nazareth?" (John 1:46). Such encouragement is beyond price.

Finally, I add a word about my present views. It is unusual to publish one's thesis more than forty years after presenting it. Inevitably, my views have changed over the years. I here briefly indicate some key differences between my views then and now.

First, I address the fundamental presupposition of this work, namely the existence of a God who is in some way identical with the God of traditional Judeo-Christian religion. Personally and philosophically, I am now much more skeptical about the existence of God than when I wrote this thesis. Having had grandchildren and a career of sorts, and even produced a few publications, I feel much less need to believe in a life after death than I once did. The need to believe in another life can arise partly from the unsatisfactory nature of one's life on earth.

Moreover, I now find that alleged "proofs" of God's existence prove far too much. I was taught that if any reality exists, then there must exist a Supreme Being, a perfect creator. But the world we know is not perfect: Its mixture of good and evil, of pleasure and pain, can be accepted as part of nature, part of the way things are. However, if the world was created by a perfect God, then on the face of things the world should be perfect, too. I know of no satisfactory answer to this argument. Indeed, such answers do little more than exclude the kind of faith that has been traditionally defended, as something fixed and certain. Even so, I do think these answers leave room for a hope, a very slight hope, that in spite of appearances there may after all be some ultimate meaning and purpose to human life, and that one day the world may indeed be perfect.

The other major doctrine that I assumed in my thesis was the existence of an "immanent" Trinity, namely three persons in God, as taught, for example, by St. Augustine and St. Thomas Aquinas. There are theologians today, both Catholic and Protestant, who hold that the Trinity is simply God's mode of self-revelation, a part of the "history of salvation," rather than a metaphysical condition of the deity itself. Against that, traditionalist Christian theologians argue cogently that a God who was a single Person would exist alone, in splendid isolation, and that the doctrine of the Trinity removes this unfortunate condition by introducing into the deity interpersonal relationships of knowledge and love. However, my thesis must be regarded as "old fashioned" on this point.

When I first formulated this theory of the incarnation in 1955, I hoped that I would be able to give the definitive interpretation of the personality of Jesus Christ, an interpretation that would be valid for time and for eternity. This was no small ambition, and it would seem to justify the effort of trying to publish the thesis with all its imperfections.

—London, September 2012

Abbreviations

DzS	H. Denzinger and A. Schonmetzer, *Enchiridion Symbolorum, definitionum et declarationum* (34th ed., Freiburg im Breisgau: Herder, 1967).
JBC	R. E. Brown, J. A. Fitzmyer, and R. E. Murphy (eds.), *The Jerome Biblical Commentary* (London: Geoffrey Chapman, 1968).
NJBC	R. E. Brown, J. A. Fitzmyer, and R. E. Murphy (eds.), *The New Jerome Biblical Commentary* (London: Geoffrey Chapman, 1997).
ST	St. Thomas Aquinas, *Summa Theologiae* (London: Eyre and Spotiswoode, 1963).
TDNT	G. Kittel (ed.), *Theological Dictionary of the New Testament* (Grand Rapids, MI: Eerdmans, 1967).
Th. Inv.	K. Rahner, *Theological Investigations*, 29 vols. (London: Darton, Longman and Todd, 1961–1992).
TWBB	Alan Richardson (ed.), *A Theological Word Book of the Bible* (London: SCM, 1956).

Introduction

Why add another book to the many already written on the incarnation? Because I think a new explanation of the incarnation is both desirable and possible.

No theological theory of the incarnation aims to be a complete explanation of the mystery. But it is possible, within the limits of human understanding, to cast more light on this central facet of Christian faith.

In the past, many explanations have come to us wrapped in the categories of ancient philosophy. Plato and Aristotle, through the work of theologians like St. Augustine and St. Thomas Aquinas, have played their part in giving meaning to the doctrine of the incarnation. But the ideas of Plato and Aristotle do not command as much respect in our modern scientific age as they once did. There is room, I think, for a model of the incarnation that takes its rise from the New Testament and the writings of the early Fathers of the church but is, at the same time, fully compatible with the modern view of man as an evolving creature in an evolving universe.

The model of *translation*, which I propose in the following pages, is, I believe, of this kind. According to this model, in Jesus Christ the eternal Word of God was translated into human flesh and form. Thus, the invisible became visible; the inaudible became audible; the intangible became tangible; and, as the climax of the whole process and the link with redemption, the impalpable became palpable.[1]

The notion of translation is used here in an *analogous* way, since we are not speaking of translation from one human language into another, but of the translation of God's eternal Word into human flesh and form. It is therefore necessary to explore the analogy by considering instances of the translation process that are most appropriate to our purpose, in particular the translation from a rich language into a poor language. In

---

1. The model was briefly treated in O'Hara, "Incarnation as Translation," (pp. 417–22) and more fully in O'Hara, "A study."

this way we may discover a hint as to why the incarnation happened just when it did in human history, and what the consequences may be for understanding it in the present stage of human development.

1

The Word Was Made Flesh

The classic place in the New Testament for the doctrine of the incarnation is John 1:14: "The Word was made flesh, he lived among us" (Greek: "pitched his tent among us"). Here the author of the Fourth Gospel states that the Logos or Word who was in the beginning with God (John 1:1) has become flesh and has come to live amongst us. The Gospel according to John is the one place in the New Testament where there is a clear statement of the incarnation of a pre-existent being. The Evangelist goes on to speak of Jesus Christ as the only Son, who is nearest to the Father's heart, and who has made himself known, that is, became God's "exegete," his translator or interpreter (Greek: *exegesato*, John 1:18).[1]

I suggest here that when the Word was made flesh, the eternal Word of God was translated into human form in Jesus Christ, so that Jesus not only became the translator or interpreter of the Father, as John 1:18 says, but was also the translation of the Father's Word into human form.

In order to give substance to this statement, I take the first four verses of the First Letter of John, which read as follows:

> Something which has existed since the beginning,
> that we have *heard*,
> and we have *seen* with our own eyes;
> that we have watched
> and *touched* with our hands:

---

1. Butler, *Why Christ*, 95, note 2: "cf. John 1:18 'No man has ever seen God, but now his only-begotten Son [i.e., Christ], who abides in the bosom of the Father, has himself interpreted God to us [i.e., is a "translation" or "rendering" of God in terms apprehensible by us; cf. "Whoever has seen me, has seen the Father," ibid. 14:9].'" The bracket insertions are Butler's.

> the Word, who is life—
> that is our subject.
> That life was made *visible*:
> we saw it and we are giving our testimony,
> telling you of the eternal life
> which was with the Father and has been made *visible* to us.
> What we have *seen* and *heard*
> we are telling you
> so that you too may be in union with us,
> as we are in union
> with the Father
> and with his Son Jesus Christ.
> We are writing this to you to make your own joy complete.
> (1 John 1:1–4; my emphases)

Here the author is speaking of the life of God made visible, so that it can be seen and heard and touched by human beings. He identifies that life with the Word or Logos. But from John, chapter 1 we know that this Word is personal, and has become flesh in Jesus Christ ("The Word was with God," John 1:1, and "The Word was made flesh," John 1:14). These four verses of 1 John 1:1–4 reveal that in Jesus Christ the invisible became visible, the inaudible became audible and the intangible became tangible. Relying on statements of the early Fathers of the church, notably Ignatius of Antioch and Irenaeus, I add that through Christ the impalpable became palpable. Thus, we can link incarnation with redemption in that through the suffering and death of Christ we get to know *who* and *what* he is.

These various aspects of the incarnation are expounded in subsequent chapters of this book. Here, I wish simply to indicate how they are rooted in the New Testament.[2]

Before moving on, however, I should note one passage of the Epistle to the Philippians that has been widely considered to denote the pre-existence of Jesus Christ. Here Paul writes:

> His state was divine,
> yet he did not cling
> to his equality with God

---

2. Confirmation comes from Bultmann, *Theology*, Vol. 2, p. 33, writing on the translation theme in 1 John 1:1–4 : "At any rate, it is clear that in the person of Jesus the transcendent divine reality became audible, visible and tangible in the realm of the earthly world."

but emptied himself
to assume the condition of a slave,
and became as men are;
and being as all men are,
he was humbler yet,
even to accepting death,
death on a cross.
But God raised him high
and gave him the name
which is above all other namesT
so that all beings
in the heavens, on earth and in the underworld,
should bend the knee at the name of Jesus
and that every tongue should acclaim
Jesus Christ as Lord,
to the glory of God the Father.
(Phil 2: 6–11)

Not all scholars view this passage as a denotation of the pre-existence of Jesus Christ. In *The New Jerome Biblical Commentary*, Brendan Byrne, SJ considers that this passage states that Christ "[as] the Godlike one 'took on' the human condition 'from outside' as it were."[3] A different opinion is expressed by James Dunn, who considers that this passage does not denote pre-existence but can be reduced to an Adam Christology. A similar view was reached independently by John Robinson.[4]

This impasse will be resolved in my subsequent chapters as I expand my previous statements taken from 1 John 1:1–4, namely that in Jesus Christ the invisible became visible, the inaudible became audible, the intangible became tangible and indeed the impalpable became palpable.

---

3. Byrne, "Philippians," 18–22.
4. Dunn, *Christology*, 114–21; Robinson, *Human Face of God*, 166.

2

The Invisible Becomes Visible

In the humanity of Jesus, the invisible Word of God is translated into visible human form. This is the first and most fundamental aspect of translation Christology. Although we can tap a rich vein of biblical theology that begins in the first chapter of Genesis, I shall first look at the main explicit statements of the theme found in the epistles of the New Testament.

The hymn in Colossians 1:15–20 describes Christ as being the head of all creation, through whom and *into* whom all things are to be reconciled. The hymn begins by proclaiming that Christ is the image of the invisible God and the firstborn of all creation, inasmuch as all things were created in him, who existed before all, and all things are to be reconciled through him and into him.

The word *eikon*, "image," occurs also at 2 Corinthians 4:4, as well as in Colossians 1:15. Here, in 2 Corinthians 4:4, Christ is described quite simply as the image of God. This passage indicates that the gospel Paul preaches is clear, but that the god of this world has blinded unbelievers and in so doing stops them from seeing the light of the gospel. This Christ "image" is the light of God that shines out of darkness, and which shines in the minds of the faithful, "to radiate the light of the knowledge of God's glory, the glory on the face of Christ" (2 Cor 4: 4–6; cf. Gen 1:3; Isa 9:1). There is also an association in 2 Corinthians 4:4 with Genesis 1:27, where man is created (male and female) in the image of God. For Paul, Christ is the Adam *intended* in Genesis.[1]

The notion of "light" brings us to the Johannine tradition. In the first chapter of this book, I quoted 1 John 1:1–4. As a reminder, this

---

1. Kittel, *TDNT,* vol. 2, 395–96.

passage sums up the first three aspects of translation Christology and also introduces the Johannine theme of life. Regarding the reference of "Word" in this passage of John, a quote from Kittel is in order: "The *logos teszoes* [Word of life] is what has been heard, seen, considered, and handled by the apostle. He goes out of his way to emphasize, in threefold repetition (vv. 1, 2, 3), the historical, spatiotemporal concreteness of what has been manifested (*ephanerothe*). It is beyond question that the *logos* is meant to be the historical figure of Jesus Christ."[2]

Cullmann, too, states that the Johannine doctrine of the Logos is an interpretation of the person of Jesus Christ.[3] Indeed, in the Prologue to the Fourth Gospel, the creative Word is seen as both life and light—"a light that shines in the dark, a light that darkness could not master"—either in the sense of "overcome" or in the sense of "grasp," "enclose," or "understand" (John 1:4–5, and the footnote in the Jerusalem Bible at John 1:5). This relates back to the creation of light and its separation from darkness as described by the priestly writer of Genesis 1:3. The author tells us that the Word was the true light, and that the world had its beginning through him (John 1:9, 10). Commenting on John 1:4, John Marsh wrote: "Light was the first gift of creation, and here the evangelist is stating that all the light of the world that brings insight and understanding to men is the work, the presence, of the Logos."[4] At this point the author has introduced Jesus as the light of the world. He will make this explicit at John 8:12 when he has Jesus proclaim "I am the light of the world."

The climax of the Prologue comes with the statement, "The Word was made flesh, he lived among us, and we *saw* his glory" (John 1:14; my emphasis). John Marsh translates the last phrase in this passage as "we have beheld his glory," and comments: "The evangelist does not shrink from using the word *beheld*, which implies that what is believed about the incarnate Word is not derived solely from spiritual insight, but is rooted also in ordinary sense perception; he will not separate "spiritual" knowledge from "sense" knowledge. The verb *beheld* is in the historic tense; he will not separate the historic events and the historic person to

---

2. Ibid., vol. 4, 127.
3. Cullmann, *Christology*, 249–69, especially 254.
4. Marsh, *Saint John*, 104.

whom he witnesses from the knowledge of the eternal God" (Marsh's emphasis).[5]

I must note two further points on this matter. The apostles bear witness to the Lord as *eye*-witnesses of his life, death, and resurrection; and the *life* that the Fourth Gospel describes as being the light of men is the life of God, a life of knowledge and love. Here knowledge is a spiritual insight, a kind of seeing, and is not sharply distinguished from love. It is knowledge by insight and connaturality rather than by conceptual reasoning.

The connection between spiritual insight and physical seeing lies in this concept: the Word becomes flesh in order that we may grasp it with the eyes of our minds. The Word is rendered into a form that becomes intelligible to us, attainable by us; this is God's way through to man, and man's way through to God.

The relation between the incarnation and creation in terms of revelation was indicated by St. Thomas Aquinas in his introduction to the treatise on the incarnation in the *Summa Theologica*. The first subject that St. Thomas treated there was the fittingness of the incarnation, and on this he wrote: "It would seem most fitting that by visible things the invisible things of God should be made known; for to this end was the whole world made, as is clear from the word of the Apostle (Romans 1:20): 'For the invisible things [of God] . . . are clearly seen, being understood by the things that are made.'"[6] Thus, the incarnation is the climax of creation, as Ephesians teaches (Eph 1:1–23). There is room for the gathering up of all things together in and under Christ as head (Eph 1:10); as well as room for the reconciliation of all things into Christ, as taught by Colossians (1:20).

Finally, the theme of *copy* or *image* occurs in the Epistle to the Hebrews, wherein we read that the Son is "the radiant light of God's glory and the perfect copy of his nature" (the express image of his substance; Heb 1:3). The character of God is to be read in Jesus. Here we see the family likeness, the Son who alone is perfect as his heavenly Father is perfect (Matt 5:48).

I may mention here that the concept of epiphany or theophany (divine appearance) is by no means confined to the Epistles and the Fourth Gospel. Central to the Gospel according to Mark are the baptism

---

5. Ibid., 109.
6. Aquinas, *ST*, 3 ,1, 1 (vol. 2, p. 2025).

of Jesus, at which he saw the heavens open and the Spirit descend upon him (Mark 1: 10), and the transfiguration, at which the apostles saw his glory (Mark 9:1–8; 2 Pet 1:18, John 1:14) and learned to believe in him (John 2:11). In John, the whole life of Jesus was a revelation of the glory that Christ had with the Father before the creation of the world (John 17: 5): God had come to dwell among men, and his glory appeared in a new Tabernacle not made with human hands, namely the Word incarnate.[7]

The Preface of the Nativity in the Roman Missal provides yet more insight into the visible mysteries of the incarnation. Here we read: "In the wonder of the incarnation your eternal Word has brought to the eyes of faith a new and radiant vision of your glory. In him we see our God made visible and so are caught up in love of the God we cannot see."[8] The Latin text of this passage provides insights that might otherwise be lost in its English translation. It states that through the incarnation we know God visibly, and so we are drawn through him to the love of things unseen. Thus it reads: "*Quia per incarnati Verbi mysterium, nova mentis nostrae oculis lux tuae claritatis infulsit: ut dum visibiliter Deum cognoscimus, per hunc in invisibilium amorem rapiamur.*" There is a happy combination of sensory and spiritual perception in the phrase "*mentis nostrae oculis,*" "the eyes of our mind." The Latin text reveals that in Christ we know God visibly, and because of this we are caught up into the love of invisible realities. Here the prayer of the church expresses the reality of the incarnation in a way that no scholastic theory could ever do.

The eye has a critical part to play in apprehending God. Beauty, no less than truth and goodness, is a divine attribute. It is a well-known psychological fact that the need to destroy beautiful things arises from the contemplation of one's own ugliness; but the destroyer, in ruining the beautiful object, destroys something in himself as well. Let us hope that a theology of the image or *eikon*, *imago Dei invisibilis*, the image of the invisible God, will help to heal some of the wounds of time and to restore Christian faith and life to unity and integrity.

I turn next to consider the second aspect of translation Christology, that in Christ the inaudible Word of God takes audible human form.

---

7. Marsh, *Saint John*, 108, commenting on the words "and dwelt among us" of John 1:14.

8. *The Sunday Missal*, 61. For the Latin text, Missale *Romanum*, 297.

3

The Inaudible Becomes Audible

In Jesus, the Word of God takes human form: the inaudible becomes audible, the ineffable is uttered; he expounds things hidden since the foundation of the world (Matt 13:55; Ps 78:2). God, having spoken at various times through the prophets, now speaks to us through his Son, through whom he made the world (Heb 1:1, 2).

Once again, this theme takes us back to the first chapter of Genesis, where God speaks and the world is made. "God said, 'Let there be light,' and there was light . . . God said . . . And so it was" (Gen 1:3, 6, 9, 11, 14, 20, 24).

Only the creation of man requires a special effort on God's part, hinted at by the priestly writer in Genesis 1: 27, and described in more detail by the Yahwist in Genesis 2:7, 21–23.

This theme of the power of God's spoken word recurs throughout the Old Testament.[1] "By the word of Yahweh the heavens were made, their whole array by the breath of his mouth . . . He spoke and it [the earth] was created; he commanded, and there it stood" (Ps 33:6, 9). "Then they called to Yahweh in their trouble and he rescued them from their sufferings; sending his word and curing them, he snatched them from the Pit" (Ps 107:19, 20).

In Psalm 147, the word of Yahweh is both active throughout nature and revealed to Israel as the Law: "He gives an order, his word flashed to earth: to spread snow like a blanket . . . he sends his word to bring the thaw. . . . He reveals his word to Jacob, his statutes and rulings to Israel" (Ps 147:15, 16a, 18a, 19).

---

1. On the theme of Jesus the Word of God, Willemse, "God's First and Last Word: Jesus," 42–53; Cullmann, *Christology*, 249–69; Bultmann, *Theology*, Vol. 2, 59–69.

The word of God is creative, effecting what it signifies: "The word that goes from my mouth does not return to me empty, without carrying out my will and succeeding in what it was sent to do" (Isa 55:11). And in the Alexandrian tradition, the Word of God can destroy as well as create: "Down from the heavens, from the royal throne, leapt your all-powerful Word; into the heart of a doomed land the stern warrior leapt" (Wisdom 18:15).

In the Jewish Wisdom writings, the Word or Wisdom of God is a hypostasis, identical with the Torah, and is both mediatrix of creation and "daughter of God" in the Rabbinic tradition.[2] The Aramaic expression *Memra Deyahweh* may be pre-Christian. At Alexandria the Word of God equals the Wisdom of God; Logos equals Sophia. Philo the Jew comes under Stoic influence; for the Stoics, the Logos was the immanent principle of order and rationality in the universe. In the Jewish Wisdom writings, Wisdom is created before the oldest of God's works; Wisdom is present at the creation, a master craftsman, delighting to be with the sons of men (Prov 8:22–26; cf. Eccl 1:1–10, 24:1–30). Wisdom is described as "a reflection of the eternal light, untarnished mirror of God's active power, image of his goodness" (Wisdom 7:26); so that the themes of Word and Image meet in Wisdom. The word of God is addressed to the heart, not merely to the ear; his light shines in the intellect, not simply in the eye.

To sum up: God's Word acts in mighty deeds; it creates and reveals, redeems and recreates. Moreover, it is eternal, ever-present to God himself; and it is personal. Now Jesus appears in the fullness of time as the one who is to fulfill God's word in the Scripture, as the one who is to speak God's word as no one ever spoke it before or since, as the one who is to stand revealed as God's eternal Word expressed in human form.

First, Jesus is the fulfillment of God's word in the Scriptures. This is the preaching of the apostles from the beginning of the church's life (Acts 2:16–36, 3:17–26). He has come to fulfill the Law as well as the Prophets (Matt 5:17–48). He is himself a Prophet,[3] the Prophet of the end times, designated at his baptism by a vision and a mission (Mark 1:10, 11). But he is more than a prophet: in Matthew 11:9 this designation is applied

---

2. Cullmann, *Christology*, 254–58. For Wisdom (Sophia) in feminist theology, Fiorenza *Jesus*, chapter 5, especially 155–62.

3. On Jesus as Prophet, Cullmann, *Christology*, 13–50; Vermes, *Jesus the Jew*, 86–102.

to the Baptist and, by implication, to Jesus himself. Because Jesus brings the final revelation of God to man, the other prophets can be called part-prophets, and Jesus can be called God's last word.[4]

As the revealer of God *par excellence*, Jesus is also the One revealed. He speaks truth, and he is the Truth; he brings light, and he is the Light; he shows the way, and he is the Way; he gives life, and he is the Life. As Cullmann says, "he brings the word, because he is the Word" (p. 259). As the Word or Logos, Jesus is more than a voice (*phone*) that cries in the wilderness (John 1:23; Isa 40:3). "The grass withers, the flower fades, but the word of our God remains forever" (Isa 40:8). Cullmann comments on the Fourth Gospel: "This is indeed the meaning of the Gospel: it intends to show that the total human life of Jesus is the center of the revelation of divine truth" (p. 260).

Thus, we come to the kernel of the Christian faith, that Jesus is not only God's last word, but his first or primeval Word as well: "Jesus is not only God's last word, but also God's first Word . . . Jesus *is* the Word of God."[5] Indeed, there are differences of interpretation among theologians, but there is no doubt about the meaning of the Gospel according to John. Thus, Bultmann writes: "Numerous formulations indicate that to John deed and word are identical," referring to John 8:28; 14:10; 15:22, 24; and "his [Jesus'] word is identical with himself."[6]

In terms of evaluating and interpreting the Johannine tradition, Bultmann insists that "Logos" comes "from a tradition of cosmological mythology" present in Judaism, in Philo, and in Gnosticism.[7] But Cullmann, rightly I think, stresses the underlying experience of Jesus of Nazareth by men: "'Logos' in the Gospel of John means the incarnate Jesus of Nazareth, the Word who became flesh, who is God's definitive revelation to the world in this human life. This is an unheard-of thought outside Christianity, even if non-Christian thinkers sometimes *say* some things about the 'Logos' which may sound the same" (p. 264; Cullmann's emphasis).

I believe that the Gospel of John arises from the concrete experience of Jesus of Nazareth by the disciples, and by the Beloved Disciple in particular. I shall say more about this in the next chapter of this book.

4. Willemse, *God's*, 50.
5. Ibid., 51 (Willemse's emphasis).
6. Bultmann, *Theology*, 60, 63.
7. Ibid., 64.

For the present, I endorse Cullmann's remark: "The universalism of the Gospel of John consists in the fact that where non-Christians spoke truth, the evangelist sees Christ, the same Christ who at a concrete, particular time became man" (p. 264).

Despite my endorsement, I would not follow Cullmann in his completely functional interpretation of Jesus as Logos. For Cullmann, the Logos is God in action; men cannot speak of the Logos apart from the action of God; abstract speculation about the natures of Christ is a useless and improper undertaking (p. 266). A full investigation of the *Logos asarkos* (the Word not in the flesh) belongs to the study of the Holy Trinity, and I shall not undertake it here. I simply note that, in my opinion, all that is positive in Cullmann's thought is taken up in my statement that Jesus is the eternal Word of God translated into human flesh and form.

Before I move on to consider the tangibility of the incarnate Word, I wish to make a point against some extreme forms of verbal religion. Christ's name is Word or Logos, and so there can be no denying or belittling that aspect of the incarnation; but an attempt to create a pure religion of the ear is, I think, a mistake. Christ never wrote a book; but he appeared, and spoke, and acted, and suffered; he was seen, and heard, and touched, and crucified, and the world could never be the same again.

The tangibility of the incarnate Word is, in a sense, even more important than his visibility and audibility. My exposition of translation Christology moves toward its climax as I turn to consider this aspect of the incarnation.

4

The Intangible Becomes Tangible

When the Word became flesh, the Word could be seen and heard and touched. Charles Davis wrote: "By the incarnation God became visible to man. He could be seen and touched. Human words conveyed divine truth and human actions became the vehicles of divine power."[1]

Karl Rahner described the incarnation as "the presence and the gradual tangibility of what God knows of himself in his divine infinity and of what he says of himself in that unbounded freedom"[2] In this context, "tangibility" is almost synonymous with "accessibility." Because the Word is there, present in Jesus, it can be grasped and apprehended and assimilated by men.

Here I recall the *locus classicus* for the tangibility of the Logos, namely 1 John 1:1-4, where the author tells of what his eyes have seen, his ears have heard, and his hands have handled of that Word who is Life. Here these three aspects of the incarnation are summed up together, reaching a climax in the statement that he has touched the Word with his hands. Tradition attributed this teaching to the disciple whom Jesus loved and who leaned on his breast at the Last Supper (John 13:23-25; 21:20, 24).[3]

Herein, I think, lies the justification of the Johannine tradition and the refutation of the doctrinaire skeptics. Attempts to see the Fourth

---

1. Davis, *Study*, 215.
2. Rahner, *Theological*, vol. 3, 31.
3. Many modern scholars think that the Beloved Disciple was not St. John the Apostle, the son of Zebedee. If the Fourth Gospel was written by the Beloved Disciple, as John 21:24 claims, he may well have been the only eye-witness among the four evangelists. Bauckham, *Jesus*, 384-411.

Gospel as a Hellenistic, pagan document have had to give way, step by step, with the progress of scholarship. The radical critics have had to keep shifting their ground, now appealing to Judaic Gnosticism, and now to the Qumran tradition. Where the Fourth Gospel was once believed to contain a very late tradition, it is now thought of in some circles as almost a pre-Christian document! In the end, the critics are left with only their prejudice that the Beloved Disciple could neither have written nor inspired these words about Jesus.

This prejudice overlooks the transforming power of love. It overlooks the intuitive, nonrational content of all knowledge, even scientific and mathematical knowledge. It ignores the extent to which perception is itself an act of love; and it overlooks the possibility that the author of the Fourth Gospel, seeing Jesus through the eyes of love, heard and remembered and understood things to which the other disciples hardly adverted. How few people take any notice of a man's words anyway! The catching phrase, the polemical utterance, yes; but the deeper realities? Is it an accident that St. Peter never quite answers Jesus' question in John 21:15, "Simon son of John, do you love me more than these others do?" By the same token, it is no accident that the Beloved Disciple stood by the cross to the end, and outran St. Peter to reach the tomb first on the morning of the resurrection (John 19:26; 20:4).

One might explore the meaning of the tangibility of the Logos throughout the Gospels. Here I note a few key points. Simeon took the infant Jesus into his arms and uttered his *Nunc dimittis*, blessing God:

> because my eyes have seen the salvation
> which you have prepared for all the nations to see,
> light to enlighten the pagans
> and the glory of your people Israel.
> (Luke 2: 30–32)

According to Mark and Luke, when the children were brought to Jesus, he asked to touch them; according to Matthew, Jesus was to lay his hands on them in prayer (Matt 19:13–15; Mark 10:13–16; Luke 18:15–17). According to Mark, "he put his arms round them, laid his hands on them, and gave them his blessing" (Mark 10:16). I must also mention the "primitive" accounts of cures given by Mark alone: namely the healing of the deaf man, when Jesus put his fingers into the man's ears and touched his tongue with spittle; and the cure of a blind man at Bethsaida, when Jesus put spittle on the man's eyes and laid his hands on him twice (Mark 7:31–37; 8:22–26). In addition, and extremely significant here, is the cure of the woman who had suffered from a hemorrhage for twelve years. Secretly she touched Jesus' clothes, and the secret bleeding stopped. But he was immediately aware that someone had touched him in a *meaningful* way; the crowd was pressing round him, but only the woman had made contact with him (Mark 5:25–34 and parallels).

Definitive for this examination of the tangibility of the Word is the episode in the house of Simon the Pharisee, narrated by Luke at 7:36–50. Here the woman who was a sinner washed Jesus' feet with her tears and dried them with her hair, kissed his feet and anointed them with ointment. In reply to Simon's unspoken criticism, Jesus both teaches him a lesson on the importance of courtesy, and points out that the woman who was forgiven much also loved much. "It is the man who is forgiven little who shows little love" (verse 47). The similar (or duplicate?) story at Mark 14:3–9 ends with the pronouncement: "I tell you solemnly, wherever throughout all the world the Good News is proclaimed, what she has done will be told also, in remembrance of her."[4]

Here our subject opens out to embrace the whole sphere of human relations, and the meaning of incarnation and redemption in human terms. This is a vast topic, too vast for me to deal with it here, and so I will restrict myself to a few general remarks. Simply, the passage should be read together with the doubtfully canonical but surely authentic pericope, John 8:1–11, about the adulterous woman. Both passages throw light on the celibacy of Jesus and its meaning in human terms.

The inability of man to integrate sex and spirit, *eros* and *agape*, is very properly the wound of sin, the place where sin "bites" into human nature. Jesus by his integrity of spirit displays also an integrity of the flesh, which then makes his flesh (and blood) our point of contact with the divine. Because Jesus embraced the children, and welcomed the attentions of the sinful woman, and accepted the love of the Beloved Disciple and St. Mary Magdalene, human flesh was transformed and sanctified. What might have been little more than an animated vegetable became the vessel of divine love. Because of the incarnation, human flesh is redeemed in principle; but the working out of this salvific process may well take centuries or even millennia.

---

4. Note that Elisabeth Schüssler Fiorenza chose the title of her first book, *In Memory of Her*, from the Marcan version of this episode.

Two scenes offer a fleeting glimpse of the glory that is to be revealed in us. Both are from the Fourth Gospel. Mary of Magdala embraces Jesus after his resurrection, and he says, "Do not cling to me, because I have not yet ascended to the Father" (John 20:17). The time for wiping away all tears had not yet come (Rev 21:4; cf. John 16:20). Thomas the twin asked to see the holes that the nails had made in Jesus' hands and to put his hand into Jesus' side. The invitation to do so was enough for Thomas to recognize the glory, and he proclaimed, "My Lord and my God!" (John 20:24–29).

The tangibility of the Word made flesh means the communication of the divine to man at all levels, including the level of the sexual and the erotic. The wound of sin is made manifest through man's inability to integrate sex and spirit, what I have called above the inability to integrate *eros* and *agape*. Let me put it this way: Our society is just as puritan as was the society of our Victorian ancestors, and perhaps a bit more so. But where the Victorians had rules about sex, rules which they often broke, our society is trying to do without the rules and make do with the primitive horror of physical contact. We are perhaps on our way to breeding a race of eunuchs. Certainly we risk losing the capacity to love and to feel compassion.

The revelation of God to man reaches its climax not merely in the tangibility of the Logos, but in his palpability: *it is by Christ's suffering and death that we get to know who and what he is*. I turn now to consider this, the central aspect of incarnational Christology, which is inseparable from redemptive Christology or soteriology.

5

The Impalpable Becomes Palpable
Atonement

An ancient and venerable formula states that in Christ the impalpable becomes palpable, the impassible becomes passible.[1] I would quarrel with the traditional view of the impassibility of God, on the basis of what the incarnation has made known to us of God's character.[2] I now insist, after Abelard, that redemption has its basis in revelation, while revelation reaches its climax in redemption. When God becomes man, we not only grasp and handle him, we also beat and crucify him, and try in vain to destroy him, to blot out the memory of his irresistible love.

Of course all this happens by God's design. St. Peter expressed it in the primitive *kerygma*, "This man, who was put into your power by the deliberate intention and foreknowledge of God, you took and had crucified by men outside the law" (Acts 2:23). Christ was delivered into the hands of men in order that by dying he might destroy our death and by rising restore our life.[3]

This part of Christian revelation has given scandal and continues to give scandal to the world. First, because people see in Christian ideas on this matter little more than a primitive doctrine of blood sacrifice. Second, because the idea of an angry God who needed to be appeased or placated by the sacrifice of his Son both attracts and repels. It attracts, hence it continues to find its defenders among well-meaning Christians;

---

1. See for example Irenaeus *Adversus Haereses* III, 16, 6: *Patrologia graeca*, 7, 925.
2. In my unpublished PhD thesis, I tried to give a metaphysical basis for the passibility of God; O'Hara, "Study," 125–35. That argument is reproduced in Appendix 1.
3. The Easter Preface in *The Sunday Missal*, 239.

The Impalpable Becomes Palpable

and it repels, hence it causes many people to number Christianity among the primitive superstitions.[4]

I will grasp the nettle here and say that I cannot accept any theory of God's appeasing or soothing himself by means of blood sacrifice. Clearly, God experiences wrath over human wickedness; clearly, the Father takes delight in his well-beloved Son. But God does not delight in suffering or in blood. In Christ, God himself grapples with sin and gets terribly hurt in the process.

First, the initiative is with God:

> Yes, God loved the world so much
> that he gave his only Son,
> so that everyone who believes in him may not be lost
> but may have eternal life.
> (John 3:16)

Second, Christ himself was God, reconciling the world to himself. Second Corinthians 5:19 states that "God in Christ was reconciling the world to himself" (Jerusalem Bible); or "God was in Christ, reconciling the world unto himself" (Authorized Version).

This astonishing fact takes us back, once again, to the beginning of Genesis. There God was at work from the dawn of creation, bringing order out of chaos, his Spirit hovering over the water (Gen 1:2). The primitive Hebrew cosmogonies saw God struggling with the powers of darkness and disorder, symbolized by the water, but reducing them to subjection by a word of command.

The same idea is latent in St. Mark's Gospel.[5] Jesus commands the winds and the sea, and they obey him. He confronts Satan in person, first in the desert and then in his ministry. Satan, the strong man of Jesus' parable, has been made prisoner by one stronger than he (Mark 3:27 and parallels); because Jesus casts out devils by the Spirit of God, the kingdom of God has already broken in (Matt 12:28; Luke 11:20).

The final confrontation is both terrible and decisive. There are two points that must be grasped here. First, God from the beginning of creation is driving out evil as light drives out darkness. Second, this is no mere Gnosis or enlightenment. Evil does not always go away when you

---

4. Feminist theologians have given a new slant to the argument by labeling this kind of scenario as "divine child abuse." Schüssler Fiorenza, *Jesus*, 98–99.

5. For these ideas in Mark's Gospel, see Nineham, *Saint Mark*.

say "Please don't!" Too often, "Please don't!" is the prelude to a murder or a rape.

These facts can best be brought home to people of our generation by looking at events nearer our own time. I consider a story that is both terrible in itself and all too typical of events in the modern world.

When Odette Hallowes, GC, had her toenails pulled out by a fellow Frenchman who was working for the gestapo, it seems to the rational mind that an act of sheer lunacy took place.[6] Clearly, she could not give the names and whereabouts of her friends and colleagues in the Resistance. But even here the mind boggles: why couldn't she give the names of her friends? The proper response to lunacy is not always obvious. But such a response is always palpable: evil has to be opposed here and now, if it is to be opposed at all. The acceptable time, the day of salvation, is always *now*; from Abraham onward, the call always comes at an awkward moment.

It is the "civilized" interrogator who adopts the "rational" approach: "Couldn't we just sit down and discuss this like sensible human beings? Then *no one need lose their toenails.*" It is the experienced procurator Pilate who says to Jesus: "Are you refusing to speak to me? Surely you know I have power to release you and *I have power to crucify you*?" (John 19:20, my emphasis). The person on the receiving end of all this sweet reasonableness is required to behave like a fanatic and provide an all-or-nothing response. Recall that all Jesus wanted to do was lead a human life, which means a life of knowledge and love: "I was born for this, I came into the world for this: to bear witness to the truth; and all who are on the side of truth listen to my voice" (John 18:37). Pilate sounds reasonable, but his question 'What is truth?' shows that in the supreme test he is not on the side of truth[7].

I believe that this line of thought is perfectly intelligible to modern men. It does not need to be reducible to rational categories, any more than life itself is reducible to rational categories. All suffering is redemptive if it is accepted in the right spirit, the spirit of Jesus who calls his betrayer "Friend!" and who prays for those who crucify him, "Father, forgive them; they do not know what they are doing" (Luke 23:34).[8] The

---

6. Tickell, *Odette*, 223.

7. Cf. Brown, *Death*, vol. 1, 752.

8. For a treatment of atonement which does not involve appeasement of an angry God, see Winter, *Atonemen*; also Hebblethwaite, "Incarnation and Atonement": "Consequently it needs to be stated quite categorically that God's forgiving love does

suffering of Jesus is not some sort of magic remedy for sin; it takes up all suffering into the supernatural life of God, and effectively completes the work of creation by translating God's invincible truth and love into the weakness of human flesh.

So the invitation to be one with God (to achieve "at-one-ment") is present in the suffering and death of Jesus. We can all reject this invitation. Individuals and societies can treat it with scorn or indifference. Let us look at this more closely here.

The rejection of Christianity arises in part from superstition or from despair. There is the superstitious belief that God, if he exists, would have to be magic, and therefore all he did would be magical. Thus, creation would have to be instantaneously perfect, and so could never require great struggle and effort to bring it to perfection. Then, there is despair that such struggle toward perfection can ever prove worthwhile. But if all suffering is redemptive, where then is the redemption? Or, put another way, how is the world different since Jesus came into it?

I believe that the difference is apparent through living faith, but only a slender thread of evidence can be pointed out to the unbeliever. There are two points to make here.

First, the fact that just because Christ has struck a decisive blow against evil does not mean that the struggle is over. The evil that followed his victory is in some ways more extreme than anything that went before: Indeed, the monstrous evil done by the Nazis under Hitler and the Communists under Stalin was greater in extent than anything the Roman pagans ever did.

Second, and this is a very subtle point indeed, the Nazis and Communists were doing evil to achieve what they regarded as a good end. That is, the post-Christian evil of the Nazis and Communists was, in its own macabre and perverted way, aimed at creating some sort of perfect society or world order. Under this mask flourished all sorts of sadism and brutality. But the whole business did not have the mindlessness of the Roman gladiatorial displays, where people were killed for amusement, literally butchered to make a Roman holiday.

It is worth noting that this last point of view is not accepted by everybody. Many people today are agnostic about all systems and ideologies, and point out that the pincers hurt just as much whether they are applied

---

not depend on the death of Christ, but rather is manifested and enacted in it." Goulder *Incarnation and Myth*, 94.

by a psychopathic criminal or a Grand Inquisitor or both in one. I go a long way with this point of view. Certainly I find a special brutality and decisiveness about the torture and burning of Giordano Bruno for heresy in the Campo dei Fiori in Rome on February 17, 1600, under the spiritual and temporal jurisdiction of the Pope. This fact is, I think, decisive for the eventual decay of both church and state in their traditional forms. The upshot is that this event fits into a Christian perspective; for when Bruno was burned, the flesh that was tortured was the flesh of Christ (cf. Matt 25:40, 45). If the human race survives on this planet for a billion years, in all likelihood there will never again be a kind of medieval church-state with all power effectively in the hands of one man.

I have dealt with only one aspect of redemption here, namely the revelational aspect. Jesus reveals himself by dying for us. He also brings atonement for our sins. But that is a vast subject which I am not discussing in this book.

I should mention that my Christology is rooted in revelation, and I would base a full soteriology on this aspect of Christ's redemptive work. Such a study is beyond the scope of this book. Even so, I should say here that I fully accept both the categories of victory and sacrifice in which the redemption has traditionally been described. Christ's victory is a victory over sin and sin's consequences, especially pain, suffering, and death. A full investigation of this aspect of the redemption would take me far from my present task, which is simply to present Christ as God's Word expressed in human form.

On sacrifice, I cannot do better than quote from William Temple: "Sacrifice is, in our experience, the noblest of spiritual qualities and the highest of known joys; and sacrifice is, for Christians, the open secret of the heart of God."[9] I simply note here that the suggestion that Christ suffered in our place (vicariously), while true (cf. John Marsh: "Peter as chief of the apostles cannot really fight his Lord's battle; rather must the Lord fight Peter's battle for him"),[10] yet does not exclude our participation in the struggle. The Pauline doctrine in Colossians is that we can, in our own bodies, try to make up all that still has to be undergone by Christ for the sake of his body, the church (Col 1:24), to that extent Christ suffered as our representative and not simply as our substitute.

9. Temple, *Christus Veritas*, 273.
10. Marsh, *Saint John*, 583.

In the light of revelational soteriology, I think that something can be said about the sinlessness of Jesus. What follows is perhaps an indirect way of seeing Jesus as Son of God and God incarnate, but it can provide a glimpse into that truth nonetheless. Let me begin by saying that I do not think that anything at all is gained by trying to speculate about the presence in Jesus' human mind of a sexual fantasy life, even though such a fantasy life appears to be a normal part of male psychology. All we need to know about this aspect of Jesus the man is that he was able to say with full conviction: "If a man looks at a woman lustfully, he has already committed adultery with her in his heart" (Matt 5:28). If we struggle with the truth of this saying, the only conclusion we can safely draw is that we are less than perfect ourselves. Let us then put aside fruitless speculation and instead concern ourselves with the all-important aspect of Jesus' sinlessness, namely his relationship to the Pharisees and the other religious leaders of his day.

Let me phrase this question openly: can Jesus be judged to have erred by the violence of his language and to have justly suffered God's condemnation, whatever the doubtfulness of the motives of those who condemned him?

I think this is very much a question of what is meant by righteousness (German, *Gerechtigkeit*; New Testament Greek, *dikaiosune*; St. Jerome's Latin, *iustitia*, justice). With deference to the scholars, I think that a key text here is Matthew 5:20, "Except your righteousness shall exceed the righteousness of the scribes and Pharisees, ye shall in no case enter the kingdom of heaven" (Authorized Version). So long as Jesus' denunciations of the scribes are looked at from the point of view that their righteousness was both true and sufficient, then Jesus can only appear to be some sort of fanatic, and probably a paranoid one at that. But once it is accepted that the Jewish scribes, and all lawyers and legal systems, are under the judgment of God—a God who searches the loins and the heart—then we can begin to see that Jesus is God's instrument who calls men to true righteousness and the circumcision of the heart.

Finally, in the famous dispute between the Thomists and the Scotists as to the purpose of the incarnation, I side unequivocally with the Thomists. As the Nicene Creed says, it was for us men and our salvation that Christ descended from heaven.[11] To speculate about what might

---

11. "Qui propter nos homines, et propter nostramsalutem, descendit de caelis." *Missale Romanum*, 224.

have happened in some other order of creation is to try to give reality to chimeras. The logical outcome of this sort of thinking would be to suggest that God can make New Year resolutions!

Next, I wish now to investigate translation theology in greater depth and to relate it to some extent to traditional thought. In order to do this, I have to consider the human heart of Jesus Christ, which is both the heart of the Word incarnate and the incarnate heart of the Word.

6

Cor Iesu Christi, Cor Verbi Incarnati, quia Cor Verbi Incarnatum

I now wish to explain in more detail what I mean by saying that, in the humanity of Jesus Christ, the Word was translated into human flesh and form. My explanation can be summed up in the phrase: "*Cor Iesu Christi, Cor Verbi incarnati, quia Cor Verbi incarnatum.*" I offer this statement as an epitome of the entire theory. Translated, this phrase means that the human heart of Jesus Christ is the heart of the incarnate Word, because it is the incarnate heart of the Word. Or, put another way: the heart of Jesus is the heart of the Word-made-flesh because it is the heart-of-the-Word made flesh.

I use the word *heart* in its biblical sense (Hebrew, *leb*) to denote the entire spiritual life, that is, knowledge, love, sentiments.[1] The life of God is a life of knowledge and love. According to my theory, the knowledge and love of God the Word or Son are summed up and expressed in the human heart of Christ. All the sentiments of the Logos toward his Father, toward the Holy Spirit, and toward the whole of creation find expression in the human heart of Jesus Christ.

The very being of the Word is thus expressed for us in the humanity of Jesus. The Word is constituted as such by being the personal knowledge or wisdom of the Father. Jesus is the personal term of the Father's divine self-knowledge, the express image of the Father's substance. It is this be-

---

1. For the meaning of *heart* (equals "mind") in the Old Testament, see *TWBB*, "Mind," 144–46; *Revue Biblique*, 31 (1922), 489–508. For the use of *heart* in St. Paul, see Bultmann, *Theology*, Vol. 1, 220–27.

ing of the Word, as Word, which is translated for us and expressed in the human heart, that is, mind, will, and emotions of Jesus Christ.

In the light of this theory, I find the clearest expression of Christ's personality in the logion given by Matthew and Luke: "No one knows the Son except the Father, just as no one knows the Father except the Son and those to whom the Son chooses to reveal him." (Matt 11:27; cf. Luke 10:22).[2] Here we find expressed the mutually exhaustive and exclusive knowledge of Father for Son and Son for Father, with only this proviso that the Son chooses to reveal the Father to others.

The entire life of Jesus is an expression of filial piety towards the Father. He repeatedly attributes unique glory to the Father. It is the burden of his message that he does not seek his own glory but the glory of the Father who sent him. Here we touch on the heart of the incarnation. Theologians such as Christian Duquoc (a Catholic) and Wolfhart Pannenberg (a Protestant), have recognized it as such.[3] Pannenberg corrected Karl Rahner on this point, showing that Rahner's basic condition of presence to the Logos should be read as a basic condition of presence to the Father. For it is by his presence to the Father, his absorption in the Father as Thou and Other, that Jesus reveals that he is the Son.

I want to stress how robust this theory is against any but the most extreme forms of higher criticism. No one who reads the Gospels with any perception can fail to see how completely Jesus was the Son of his heavenly Father. Even liberal Protestantism sought to make the belief in the Fatherhood of God and the brotherhood of men the basic minimum of Jesus' teaching. Wherever you turn in the Gospels you find Jesus referring to God as his Father. From the Sermon on the Mount to the Johannine discourses, Jesus teaches and preaches his heavenly Father. The

---

2. Perhaps I should indicate briefly my attitude to the Gospels as history. This is a vast topic that becomes ever more subtle with the progress of biblical scholarship. Of course it is known that the Gospels express the faith and preaching of the church (the *kerygma*). The historicity of the Fourth Gospel presents special problems because of its probable date of composition (about 95 CE) and because of the elaborate theological discourses that it attributes to Jesus. My own attitude is to accept as valid the interpretation that this Gospel gives of the personality of Jesus, and not worry too much about whether any particular sentence gives the actual words of Jesus. At the same time, I realize the need to inform myself as far as possible of the current critical status of every periscope that I use in my work. Note that I use the names Matthew, Mark, Luke, and John for the four Gospels without assuming that the actual authors had those names.

3. Duquoc, *Christologie*; Pannenberg, *Jesus*.

Gospel according to Mark, for example, contains this carefully graded statement: "But as for that day or hour, nobody knows it, neither the angels of heaven, nor the Son; no one but the Father" (Mark 13:32). Mark also gives the implicitly powerful reference by way of the parable about the wicked husbandmen who killed the beloved son and heir in order to gain the inheritance for themselves (Mark 12:1–12).[4] Indeed, Mark's Gospel is apparently introduced as the Good News about Jesus Christ the Son of God (Mark 1:1). Near the end of the Gospel, the centurion says, "In truth this man was a son of God" (Mark 15:39). Beyond the Gospels, one only has to look to St. Paul for guidance in these matters: God is the Father of Our Lord Jesus Christ; God's proper name is Father, and the proper source of paternity is God (Eph 3:15).

At this point I must refer to biblical theology that concerns the title Son of God (*huiostou Theou*). This is a vast topic that I can barely touch on here.[5] I will merely note that Modernists like Loisy, who wished to reduce this "Son of God" title to a messianic title, rather missed the point; Jesus' filial consciousness was at the root of his personality and is far more fundamental to him than are any sociopolitical connotations, such as that of Messiah or Christ. Jesus is the Christ because he is the Son of God, not vice versa. As Oscar Cullmann has written, "The conviction that in a unique way he was 'God's Son' must belong to the very heart of what we call the self-consciousness of Jesus."[6] I shall return to this point later.

Unexpected confirmation of the centrality of Jesus' sonship can be gleaned from recent German theology. Thomas E. Clarke, SJ, referring to Gogarten's work, has written: "Friedrich Gogarten's 'mature sonship' beautifully expresses the touching paradox contained in the Gospel Christ: the most creative and adult personality the world has ever seen, the man who has most decisively influenced human history going about with the word 'Father' constantly on his lips, and looking continually to that Other as source of his very creativity."[7] Christianity has placed personality at the center of the stage of human history because of the unique

---

4. I accept Raymond Brown's distinction between what Jesus knew of his divinity and whether he might not have been able to express what he knew. Brown, *Introduction*, 203–4.

5. Cullmann, *Christology*, 270–305.

6. Ibid., 282.

7. Clarke, "Humanity of Jesus," 2, 241.

filial personality of Jesus, which is completely grounded in the personality of God his Father.

I have said that all the sentiments of the Logos toward his Father, toward the Holy Spirit, and toward the whole of creation find expression in the human heart of Jesus Christ. Only on the eve of his death did Jesus give clear expression to his relationship with the Holy Spirit:

> Still, I must tell you the truth:
> it is for your own good that I am going
> because unless I go,
> the Advocate will not come to you;
> but if I do go,
> I will send him to you . . .
> He will glorify me,
> since all he tells you
> will be taken from what is mine.
> Everything the Father has is mine;
> that is why I said:
> All he tells you
> will be taken from what is mine.
> (John 16:7, 14, 15)[8]

Only as the disciples lived in the Christian community formed by the Holy Spirit did they come to savor Christ's gift to them and to understand that their new Friend and Counselor was no less personal than the man called Jesus who had sent the Holy Spirit to them. But I do not wish to develop this theme now. I will treat explicitly of the Holy Spirit in chapter 14.

The solicitude of the Logos for mankind and indeed for the whole of creation is expressed in Jesus' life of dedication and in his preaching, especially in the parables and the Sermon on the Mount. Often it is of the Father's concern that he speaks, a concern that Jesus clearly shares.

> Can you not buy two sparrows for a penny? And yet not one falls to the ground without your Father knowing. Why, every hair on your head has been counted. So there is no need to be afraid; you are worth more than hundreds of sparrows."

---

8. Schillebeeckx, *Christ the Sacrament*, 42. "Passover and Pentecost are the interpretation on the human plane of the divine relations of Son to Father, and of the Son in unity with the Father to the Holy Spirit." Note that in quoting from the Farewell Discourse in John 16 I must allow for the possibility that these are the author's words, written from a post-resurrection perspective, and not necessarily the words of Jesus himself. See note 2.

Cor Iesu Christi, Cor Verbi Incarnati, quia Cor Verbi Incarnatum

(Matt 10:29–31)

> Look at the birds in the sky. They do not sow or reap or gather into barns; yet your heavenly Father feeds them. Are you not worth much more than they? . . . Think of the flowers growing in the fields; they never have to work or spin; yet I assure you that not even Solomon in all his regalia was robed like one of these."
> (Matt 6:26, 28b, 29)

Through the acts of teaching, healing, and sanctification, the life of Jesus is one of dedication to the needs of his fellow men. This is summed up in the passage that he read from Isaiah at Nazareth:

> The spirit of the Lord has been given to me,
> for he has anointed me.
> He has sent me to bring the good news to the poor,
> to proclaim liberty to captives
> and to the blind new sight,
> to set the downtrodden free
> to proclaim the Lord's year of favor.
> (Luke 4:18–19; Isa 61:1–2)[9]

Jesus deals with people by meeting them where they are, with full respect for their individuality and human dignity. If his very presence makes Pilate seem like an extra in the drama of human salvation, Pilate is not robbed of his dignity or reduced to caricature. "You would have no power over me if it had not been given you from above; that is why the one who handed me over to you has the greater guilt" (John 19:11).

It is the same in every situation; there are harsh words, words that take account of the real situation of the moment, while tempered with compassion and love. The parables show a vast range of sympathy with every possible human predicament. Even the rich man tormented in Hades is allowed to make his very human request for a drop of water, although the request is not granted (Luke 16:24–26). Here again a climax is reached in the prayer after the Last Supper. Jesus expresses the love that is to be mediated to us by those whom he sends on his errand:

---

9. Note that this passage, placed by Luke at the start of Jesus' public ministry, is a program for a liberation theology if ever there was one! On its historicity, see Meier, *Marginal Jew*, vol. 1, 269–71, 302–3.

> They do not belong to the world
> any more than I belong to the world.
> Consecrate them in the truth;
> your word is truth.
> As you sent me into the world,
> I have sent them into the world,
> and for their sake I consecrate myself
> so that they too may be consecrated in truth.
> (John 17:16–19)

We notice here how all the other relationships of Jesus, to the Holy Spirit and to the world, are founded on and rooted in his relationship to his Father, just as our relationship to the Father is rooted in Jesus' relationship to the Father (John 20:17b). We may listen to Schillebeeckx here: "In and through the liturgical mystery of worship that is his sacrifice on the Cross, against the background of the whole of his life in God's service, the being of the Son of God as 'from the Father' and 'to the Father,' is fully revealed and realized on the human plane of his sonship."[10]

Both Catholic and Protestant piety, following the early Fathers of the church, have seen in the heart of Jesus the symbol of his divine and human love. The heart is certainly not the seat of the emotions, which technically are localized in the brain. Rather, the heart is both a natural and a conventional symbol of emotion; it is a natural symbol, because it reacts in a natural way to the presence of emotion and so becomes a sign of that emotion. In a similar way, my Christology relates explicitly to the human heart of Jesus Christ as the symbol of his love.

Monsignor Ronald Knox in a sermon entitled "The Perfect Flowering of a Human Life" (preached on June 17, 1956, at Chorlton-cum-Hardy, Manchester) said: "And that is the real meaning of the Sacred Heart devotion; it translates the Divine Nature into human terms for us."[11] Here the translation theme is explicitly present, centered on the heart of Jesus. More simply the New Catechism introduced by the Bishops of the Netherlands in 1967 said, "The human heart of Christ is the heart of God."[12]

By a happy combination, three aspects of this theory, namely revelation centered in the heart of Jesus as the secret of redemption, are brought

---

10. Schillebeeckx, *Christ the Sacrament*, 37. I refer, too, to Nédoncelle, "Le moi du Christ," Bouëssé and Latour, *Problèmes* 201–26. See, too, Galot, *La Personne*, 75–119.

11. *Tablet* (June 30, 1956), 614.

12. *New Catechism*, 81.

Cor Iesu Christi, Cor Verbi Incarnati, quia Cor Verbi Incarnatum

together in a verse of the hymn *Cor arca legem continens*, appointed to be read on the Feast of the Sacred Heart of Jesus and contained in the Roman Breviary:

> *Te vulneratum caritas*
> *Ictu patenti voluit,*
> *Amoris invisibilis*
> *Ut veneremur vulnera.*

This may be translated: "Love willed that You [the heart of Jesus, here personified] be wounded with a blow that disclosed its secrets, in order that we might revere the wounds of the love we cannot see."[13] Here the invisible becomes visible, the impalpable becomes palpable, and the secret of infinite love is read, symbolically, in the open heart of Jesus Christ. The fine sentence of Charles Davis is most appropriate here: "Christ was the sacrament of the divine love, and the radiant center of the living symbol was his heart with its depths of charity."[14]

This same theme is present in Anglican and Protestant writers, too. William Temple wrote: "The Incarnation is an episode in the Life or Being of God the Son; but it is not a mere episode, it is a revealing episode. There we see what He who is God's wisdom always is, even more completely than any Kenotic theory allows. This view makes the humiliation and death of Christ 'the measure of that love which has throbbed in the divine heart from all eternity.'"[15]

Karl Barth, in his last complete work, had this to say: "If Jesus Christ is the Word of Truth, the 'mirror of the fatherly heart of God' (Martin Luther), then Nietzsche's statement that man is something that must be overcome is an impudent lie. Then the truth of God is, as Titus 3:4 says, His loving-kindness and nothing else."[16]

I would like to stress that the theory of the incarnation that I am putting forward here points to the Gospels for its justification. The word *translation* itself is, I think, as close to John 1:18 as the word *incarnation* is to John 1:14. Moreover, this theory does not rest on any metaphysical abstraction but on a detailed and loving examination of the words and

---

13. *Hours of the Divine Office*, vol. 2, 1526.
14. Davis, *Study of Theology*, 240.
15. Temple, *Christus*, 144.
16. Barth, *Humanity*, 49.

deeds of Jesus as recorded for us in the Gospels. This reminder is critical for relating this translation Christology to traditional thought.

By "traditional thought," I mean the doctrine that Jesus Christ is "truly God and truly man." In the Council of Chalcedon, a formulation was reached that described Jesus as one divine person with two natures, the divine nature and a human nature. I realize that support for the "two natures" doctrine of Chalcedon has waned, even among moderate theologians.[17] In fact I would claim that translation Christology is Chalcedon-compatible rather than Chalcedon-dependent, and that it avoids the absurdities that some traditionalist exponents of Chalcedon defend.

The main point that I wish to make here is that translation Christology does not merely present Jesus as a translation of the Word into human form and therefore, it could be argued, as nothing more than a man. Instead, it accepts him as the Word expressed in human form, and agrees with the traditional formulation that his humanity is hypostatically united to the eternal Word of God.

To explain this, I define the formal constituent element of the hypostatic union to be the Word-consciousness of Jesus. This Word-consciousness was something that existed in his human mind, something by means of which he was taken up into the personality of the Word, so that he was not a human person in his own right, but subsisted in the Word, with the subsistence of the Word and no other.

I distinguish at once between Word-consciousness and Word-contemplation.[18] The position of Nestorius, as rejected in the Council of Ephesus in the year 431, was that Jesus and the Word were two distinct persons. Indeed, the man Jesus was intimately united to the Word in a moral union. For the sake of clarity I call this kind of inadequate union Word-contemplation. I am defending something quite different here, namely Word-consciousness, that is, the consciousness of *being* the Word expressed in human form. Now you can contemplate the Word forever without becoming the Word. What I defend is something different: it is Word-consciousness, that is, the consciousness of *being* the Word expressed in human form.

---

17. For a balanced approach to Chalcedon, see Macquarrie, *Jesus Christ*, 385.

18. When Schleiermacher spoke of the "God-consciousness" of Jesus, he meant what I would call "God-contemplation." Some modern theologians refer to an "Abba-consciousness" of Jesus in this sense. [See Schleiermacher, *Faith* , p. 385.]

Cor Iesu Christi, Cor Verbi Incarnati, quia Cor Verbi Incarnatum

Strictly speaking, the emphasis here should be on Son-consciousness rather than on Word-consciousness. We might even, along with Oscar Cullmann, talk about a *Pais*-consciousness of Jesus, where the Greek word *Pais* is close to the Hebrew *ebed* and to the German *Knecht*. It connotes loving obedience on the part of Jesus, the Servant of Yahweh and well-beloved Son of his heavenly Father; obedience even unto death, the death of the cross. "In this respect it would be even more correct to speak of a Pais-consciousness of Jesus than of his messianic consciousness."[19] But I use the term *Word-consciousness* in order to designate Jesus as the Word or Logos. The nearest actual Gospel account of Word-consciousness as such can be discerned in the Sermon on the Mount, in which Jesus adds to and perfects the God-given Mosaic law using the phrase, "But I say this to you" (Matt 5:22, 28, 32, 34, 39, 44). This is no prophetic utterance but the very oracle of God.[20]

An objection could be put forth, especially by traditionalist scholastic theologians, on the grounds that the phenomenon of Word-consciousness could only affect the human nature of Jesus accidentally, and not substantially, or rather subsistentially, in the order of subsistence, on the ultimate level or plane of existence. The answer to this objection depends on the attitude adopted to such Aristotelian concepts as "substance" and "accident" (i.e., "accidental" or "nonessential" quality or property) and to the further concepts of "nature," "essence," and "subsistence," arising from Greek philosophy and used in the early councils of the Christian church. (I have added a note on such Aristotelian—and scholastic—concepts at Appendix A of this book). Without wishing to be too technical, I would just say here that the sixteenth century neoscholastic interpretations of Aristotle's categories were, in my opinion, flawed by exaggerated realism. An important corrective was given by Immanuel Kant, who saw that these categories depend on the operation of the human mind.[21]

One does not have to follow Kant into the cul-de-sac of idealism in order to realize that categories like "substance" and "accidental quality" are not distinct realities but aspects of reality distinguished by the

---

19. Cullmann, *Christology*, 80–81.

20. The consciousness which Jesus has of being the Word expressed in human form is much more explicit in the Gospel of John than in the Synoptic Gospels. Note that my theory does not require this consciousness to be permanent and continuous. It can and does have its climactic moments.

21. Kant, *Critique*, e.g., 308–14.

human mind. It may be convenient to think of water, for instance, as a "substance," with its "qualities" like wetness and so on; but a sufficient modification of the "qualities" of water (e.g., by electrolysis) will change it into hydrogen and oxygen.

The consequence for incarnation theory is that it can be argued that if a man's consciousness is absorbed into a higher consciousness, then his human nature is no longer a human person in its own right but has been taken up and assumed by a superior person.

I do not wish to labor this point unduly. Translation Christology does not start from a "two natures" position, and it does not risk the kind of absurdity sometimes associated with that position, for example, when reputable theologians argue that Jesus had two minds, and further that he knew some things with one mind and did not know them with the other mind! That is a doctrine of "split personality" if ever there was one, and runs counter to the unity of the person of Jesus that Chalcedon was so anxious to maintain.[22]

A further comment is needed here. Notice the creative role of consciousness, which is not a purely passive awareness of something that already is the case, but an active awareness of the self in confrontation with others and as involved in a network of relationships that are dynamic, not static. On the human plane, Jesus creates his personality like any other man; but he is perfectly responsive to the creative activity of God within his human frame.

Note further that translation Christology, in its positive exposition, enjoys a transparent simplicity. The most primitive peoples often speak more than one language or dialect. They can easily understand what a translation is, much in the way they understand a family likeness. I have had to develop the theory along rather abstract lines in this chapter in order to do justice to the formulas of traditional theology.

But this very simplicity of translation Christology can be the source of another objection. Where, it may be asked, is the *mystery* of the incarnation, attainable by faith alone, and impervious to reason? I reply that the mystery of the incarnation most certainly does not consist in some sort of metaphysical trick performed on Christ's essence and existence, which would imply that God incarnate might, without metaphysical contradiction, have been a monstrous sinner or a lunatic. No, the incarnation

---

22. Nine times the main decree of Chalcedon affirms the unity of "Our Lord Jesus Christ." DzS, 302 (148).

Cor Iesu Christi, Cor Verbi Incarnati, quia Cor Verbi Incarnatum is the mystery of God revealed in Christ. It is the mystery kept hidden from the beginning of time in the all-creating mind of God (Eph 3:9). It is the mystery contained in every page of the Gospel story, not least in Christ's obedience-in-disobedience and disobedience-in-obedience even unto death (cf. Matt 23:2–3; Mark 12:17; 14:62; John 18:37; Mark 14:36).

I refer again to William Temple, writing about the divinity of Christ: "We have not here a perplexing dogma imposed by authority upon men's reluctant minds; what we have is a triumphant discovery based on experience as all scientific truth must be based."[23] But I note that the mystery of the incarnation is impervious to reason because the mystery of the Holy Trinity is impervious to reason. The Trinity is not only the mystery *par excellence*; it is the fundamental mystery in Christianity, implicit in all the other mysteries. It is the unique supernatural object that gives to the theological virtues and hence to the cardinal virtues their supernatural status.

Finally, I must note that translation Christology requires a very "high" interpretation of certain passages in the New Testament, passages often given a "low" or minimalist interpretation by critical scholars. I shall return to this point in a subsequent chapter when I consider the phenomenon of christogenesis.

---

23. Temple, *Christus*, 112.

7

Technical Aspects of Translation Christology

Because I am putting forward the concept of "translation" as a reinterpretation of Christology, it is important to look at both the advantages and the limitations of this concept. Clearly the term translation is being used in an analogous fashion. The finite analogue consists in the translation of a word or series of words from one human language into another. The infinite analogue consists in the translation of the eternal Word of God into human form. There are differences and similarities here between the finite and the infinite analogues that need closer examination.

The *difference* is that the result of the translation process is not a word or series of words but a human nature hypostatically united to the eternal Word of God. It is not then a question of translating one finite word into another word, or even the infinite Word of God into a single finite word. The analogy with ordinary translation is therefore imperfect in the end result, or term, of the translation process. Indeed, the word "translation" is suggested, not by the end result of the process but by John 1:18, which shows Jesus Christ as the interpreter or translator of God, and by the fact that it is a Word, the eternal Word of God or Logos, which is being expressed in human form.

This imperfection in the analogy is not fatal to the theory because a *personal* Word is here being expressed in human form. The richness of the Word of God means that this Word is a person and not a thing. Hence an appropriate expression for the Word of God cannot be found in a mere word or collection of words.

The Word of God has to be expressed through the medium of a human nature, and with all that this implies in terms of consciousness and personality. A personal expression is required for the personal Word of God because God's Word is also God's Son, who can be expressed in created form only through the medium of a human filial consciousness.[1]

A second and more basic difference is that human languages operate approximately on the same level with each other. Making due allowances for differences of experience and culture, we can expect to find a word in one human language that is equivalent to a word in another human language.[2] Even if this is not true of individual words, it may be true of sentences and whole treatises, especially where these sentences or treatises are factual and scientific rather than imaginative and poetic. But it is not clear that any created expression could ever be equivalent to the infinite Word of God, in any sense at all. This is a problem that will require detailed treatment. I shall consider it later under Calvin's phrase, *Finitum non capax infiniti*: The finite is not capable of the infinite.

The *similarity* between human translation and the divine translation lies in this: Both are concerned with the communication of meaning. Translation is a branch of linguistics, and has the same purpose as language itself, namely the communication of meaning, beauty, and experience. We translate in order to make an author's meaning available to a wider public, namely those who cannot read the language of an original work.

All of these purposes are included in the purpose of God's activity, which is self-communication in love. Both "inside" and "outside" of the Trinity, God wishes to communicate himself, to bestow his own goodness, by communicating meaning, life, beauty, love, and the experience of love. We must, therefore, consider the technical problems associated with translation as the communication of meaning, especially when meaning is translated from a richer language into a poorer language, or is translated to a people of a totally alien culture ("radical translation"). I shall consider these problems in my next chapter.

---

1. The application of the masculine terms "Father" and "Son" to the deity is, of course, historically conditioned. It should not be confused with the biological maleness of Jesus' human nature.

2. A striking exception is provided by Eskimo, which has no word for "sheep," since the Eskimo do not keep sheep. The Biblical phrase "lamb of God" has to be translated for the Eskimo as "seal of God." See Brower, *On Translation*, 279.

A study of the technical aspects of human translation leaves unresolved the question whether it is possible, even in principle, for God to translate his divinity into human form. It will therefore be necessary to consider to what extent man is capable of God or, in Luther's phrase, *Finitum capax infiniti:* the finite is capable of the infinite. An entry to this notion is provided by the biblical teaching that man is made in God's image (Gen 1:27). We might therefore expect humanity to be radically capable of expressing divinity, whereas some other natures (for example, the nature of a cow) could not. Of course this radical capacity is founded in God's creative action in forming man's nature and is no more that a human openness to God ("obediential potency") that is when God deigns to reveal himself to man in and through human nature.

In the next chapter, I shall therefore consider translation as such, and then the capacity in man for expressing divinity. Finally, I shall return to the basic problem of trying to express the infinite in the finite; and, once again, I shall rely on the Gospel evidence rather than on any *a priori* notion as to what it might or might not be possible for God to do.

8

Translations as the Communication of Meaning

The concept of translation might be approached either in an abstract or a concrete way. I shall adopt an abstract approach. First I will look at *radical translation* and *automatic translation* in order to isolate some of the basic ingredients of the process. I will then turn to *poetic translation* and *religious translation*, paying particular attention to the problem of translating religious notions from a richer to a poorer language.

Radical translation has been defined by the logician Willard V. Quine as "translation of the language of a hitherto untouched people."[1] Quine envisages the situation in which an English linguist goes into the jungle to learn the language of a completely unknown tribe. In practice, of course, our linguist would live with the natives until he became completely bilingual, and would then compose a dictionary. (This situation provides an interesting analogy with the incarnation; Jesus spent about thirty years learning to be a man before he began to translate God into human terms for us.) But it is more useful, in a study of radical translation, to consider how the linguist might gain his first insights into the meanings of native terms.

In an article entitled "Meaning and Translation" (148–72), Quine adopts a carefully empirical approach. If the linguist points to a rabbit and says, "Rabbit," and if the native says "Gavagai," how is the linguist to know whether the term "Gavagai" actually means "Rabbit"? Quine easily shows that this problem is insoluble; terms are inscrutable. "Gavagai" might

---

1. Brower, *On Translation*, 148. All page references in this chapter up to note 6 are to this work.

in theory mean "mere stages, or brief temporal segments, of rabbits." It might mean "all and sundry undetached parts of rabbits" (153). Initially, there would be no way for the linguist to tell.

Instead of examining terms, Quine therefore looks at sentences. He takes "Rabbit!" to mean "This is a rabbit." He defines an *occasion sentence* (as distinct from a *standing sentence*) as one that commands assent or dissent only as prompted all over again by current stimulation (150). He thus arrives at a concept of the *stimulus meaning* of a sentence as the ordered pair of the classes of all the stimulations that would prompt the native to assent to or to dissent from the sentence. For example, if all possible stimuli were restricted to isolated numbers from the set (1, 2, 3, . . . , 10) then the stimulus meaning of the sentence "Even number!" would be the class (2, 4, 6, 8, 10) followed by the class (1, 3, 5, 7, 9). Quine observes: "Occasion sentences and stimulus meaning are general coin, whereas terms, conceived as variously applying to objects in some sense, are a provincial appurtenance of our object-positing kind of culture" (154–55).

The theory so far applies to each native informant taken separately; each has his own set of stimulus meanings for occasion sentences. In order to generalize the theory, it is necessary to take account of *collateral information*, such as would be used in assenting to the occasion sentence "Bachelor!"(155). Quine therefore defines *observation sentences* as those that do not depend on collateral information; more precisely, he says that an observation sentence is an "occasion sentence producing intersubjective stimulus meaning"; that is, it will have the same stimulus meaning for a wide class of native informants. In fact, it is easy to see that the translation of occasion sentences by stimulus meanings will only work for observation sentences; this is automatic.

Quine next considers what he calls the *intrasubjective synonymy* of occasion sentences. Such sentences are here called *synonymous* if they are alike in stimulus meaning for the given subject. An example from one language is the pair of sentences "Bachelor!" and "Unmarried man!" A bilingual person will have intrasubjective synonymy for sentences in the two languages. As I have already remarked, this is how a translator would in fact work; he would make himself bilingual, learning the other language "like a native."

Besides observation sentences, Quine notes that the simplest *truth functions*, such as "Not," "And," and "Or" can be simply translated in terms of stimulus meaning. For example, "Not" changes assent into dissent and dissent into assent. But the whole class of sentences that are neither observation sentences nor truth functions appear to require methods that do not yield to precise rational analysis. There will be a technique of trial and error, which Quine calls the formation of *analytical hypotheses.*

These hypotheses, he notes, are not unique, in the sense that contradictory hypotheses can be supported from all the available evidence (170). He notes that "containment in a continuum of cultural evolution" facilitates "translation from Hungarian into English," for example (170). Finally, he remarks that "there is less basis of comparison—less sense in saying what is good translation and what is bad—the farther we get away from sentences with visibly direct conditioning to nonverbal stimuli and the farther we get off home ground" (172).

Quine's analysis of radical translation in terms of stimulus meaning is very useful in highlighting the importance of shared experience as the basis of the communication of meaning. For my purposes here, it would have been quite impossible for God effectively to translate his Word into human form unless men had some experience of God on which to base their recognition of Jesus. This fact is recognized in Catholic teaching about the *praeparatio evangelica*, or preparation for the Gospel, both inside and outside of Judaism. A full investigation of this would need to acknowledge the detailed and loving care with which God had to implant the knowledge of God in men's hearts before he could introduce the Logos into the world. An understandable desire to emphasize the uniqueness of the Christian revelation can blind Christians to the fact that men cannot truly understand any word at all except on a basis of shared experience. The experience of God in Judaism and in Hellenism was clearly of fundamental importance for an effective translation of God's Word into human form. There is no basis for supposing that the precise confession of Thomas, "My Lord and my God!" (John 20:28) could ever have arisen in any other historical and cultural context.

The "pure" or abstract concept of translation might be expected to appear clearly in the context of automatic or machine translation. As Anthony G. Oettinger points out, machine translation is a matter of finding precisely defined rules for substituting words or phrases in one language for words or phrases in another language.[2]

---

2. Oettinger, in an article topically entitled "Automatic (Transference, Translation, Remittance, Shunting)," The title of this article was supplied by a machine! From Brower, *On Translation*, pp. 240–67.

The difficulty in finding such rules arises chiefly from "the need for explicit specification of the *characteristics of the context*" (241). In fact one is confronted with the almost infinite variety of meanings that most or all words or phrases can take according to their context. Machine translation becomes possible and practicable only when there are sufficient cases in which a word or phrase requires the same translation and when these cases can be recognized and isolated in a reasonable number of logical steps.

This task is not quite as hopeless as it sounds, because "an important aspect of meaning can be preserved over quite a range of variation in formal structure" (250). Oettinger cites an example of two consecutive translations, from English into French and back again (i.e., English–French–English–French–English) by four different people, leading to a great alteration of style, but very little change of meaning. Perhaps we should set against this the experiment in which translation from Danish into Swedish, German, English, French, and finally Danish again, resulted in a final product that was unrecognizable from its original (282).

In any case, it is clear that the purpose of automatic translation is "not to charm or delight . . . but to be of wide service in the work-a-day task of making available the essential content of documents in languages which are foreign to the reader" (266). Automatic translation is clearly useful in the sciences. But there is little or no room for automatic translation when it comes to translating poetry or religious concepts, to which I now turn.

It is agreed that the translation of *poetry* involves more than the mechanical communication of meaning, and that some sort of transmission of style is essential. It is also well agreed that style cannot be slavishly imitated, but that the translator of poetry must write a poem of his own, seeking to give readers the same sort of experience as the original work gave him. Outside of these two points there is very little agreement about method or standards in translating poetry.

The extreme view is expressed in the Italian proverb *Traduttore–traditore*: the translator is a traitor. The same point is made in the traditional likening of translations to mistresses; they cannot be both beautiful and faithful. T. F. Higham wrote: "All translation is a kind of illusion . . . Those translations are always best in which the illusion is most complete and the idiom seems least suggestive of translation."[3]

3. Preface to Oxford book of Greek verse in translation (London, 1938); quoted from Brower, 285.

Some fundamental points were made by Eugene A. Nida, writing about Bible translating (11–31). "There are no complete synonyms, that is to say, words which may substitute for each other in all possible positions of occurrence" (25); all we can say is that "some words are substantially identical with others." By the same token, "absolute communication is quite impossible," but "close approximations" may be obtained (31). The danger latent in word-for-word translation is forcibly illustrated by the rather sinister fact that "in some languages of the Congo . . . 'heap coals of fire on one's head' was seen as an excellent new means of torturing people to death" (29).

Poetry is in a class apart since, in the words of Valéry, the poet "translates ordinary speech, modified by emotion, into 'language of the gods'" (74). It follows that, in order to translate poetry, we need "not a representation, in any formal sense, but a comparable experience" (34).

Opinions differ as to how far the translator of poetry should even try to reproduce the original poem. Thus Douglas Knight, writing about the Augustan translators, especially Pope (196–204) says: "He [the translator] will not translate to make a poem available in his own language for those who cannot read the original, but rather to express a kind of insight which many of his audience can interpret in the composite matrix of their world and of that of the original" (198). Other people have stressed the need to make the original intelligible, which will normally mean translating poetry into prose. Jackson Matthews, having "Third Thoughts on Translating Poetry" (67–77), suggests that verse should be translated into both verse and prose, and that the verse translation should be placed first, followed by the original with a facing prose translation (77).

Very little of this is directly applicable to my theme. However, if we press the analogy of the translation of poetry as the "language of the gods," we could say that we might expect the human translation of the divine Word to be utterly human, fully creative, and even idiosyncratic as a human personality, but at the same time to bear the stamp of divine greatness. This is very much what we find in the Gospels.

Some other remarks of our authors (and translators) are extremely relevant. Richard Lattimore, a translator of Greek poetry, writes that "context is all," and that "no translator . . . can escape being colored by his own time . . . One cannot translate in a vacuum" (53–54).

These remarks are very relevant to an understanding of Jesus. Of course we must remember too that God prepared the context of the incarnation, which is therefore, *within the bounds of metaphysical possibility*, under his control. Jacques Barzun has pointed out that the translator must have two minds with twin thoughts (289); this reflection is very apt for traditional two-nature Christology, viewed in the light of translation Christology.

But the most interesting applications of translation theory to our subject arise when it is a question of translating from a richer language into a poorer language. This is especially true when it is the whole richness of some cultural expression that is involved. I shall consider here how, according to Douglas Knight, Pope aimed at capturing Homer's *heroic insight*, in spite of the gulf between Pope's world and Homer's.

As an aside, I feel it important to note the interesting point made by Renato Poggioli: "How many mystics or symbolists have claimed that even original poetry is a form of translation, an attempt to rephrase the heavenly music that many can no longer hear in the noisy chaos of this world!" (144).

Douglas Knight stresses the importance of Pope's seven years of encounter with Homer. Pope had to subordinate his own poetic insight "to the demands and world view, not only of a far greater artist but one who was different from himself in many crucial ways" (200). Pope had therefore to mediate between two worlds, to immerse himself in the "other" world and act imaginatively as though it were the central one, without losing his interest in his own world. The challenge of Homer to Pope was the double one of apprehending the direct experience of final realities and of "somehow bringing it to bear on the infinite nuances and indirections of a conventionally sophisticated world" (199).

The cultural contrast between Homer's world of stark and final realities and Pope's world of trivial and frivolous detail is a useful analogy for my purpose. The total simplicity of God is in sharp contrast with the diversity and the distraction of multiplicity present in the created world. The Johannine revelation of Christ's life with the Father could seem "empty" to Rudolf Bultmann,[4] just because of the apparent "emptiness" or "poverty" of God. The "poverty" of God consists in his simplicity, which is rich in meaning but cannot be directly apprehended by man, except through the kind of single-minded vision of God that Jesus possessed and which he came to share with us.

---

4. Bultmann, *Theology*, 59–61.

I note too that according to Douglas Knight, Pope's work on Homer brought him to a poetic maturity that would not have been possible to him otherwise (200–201). This interesting claim corresponds to the fact that Jesus, as God the Son in human form, was the most mature human personality the world has ever known.

Before moving on to consider religious translation, I feel it important to note some remarks of John Hollander concerning the difference between a *version* and a *translation*. A translation, Hollander says, is always *interpretive*; hence a vindication of the rightness and unique propriety of a translation amounts to a *persuasive* assertion that this is the case. For Christian and Catholic faith, this corresponds to the fact that the acceptance of Jesus as our Lord and our God by personal faith enters into, and in some sense *constitutes*, the existence of Jesus as God *for us*. This acceptance is contingent on the fact that we have either walked with Jesus on the way, as Thomas and the other disciples did, or have stood in some relation to the community initiated by those who did walk with him. Christians who fail to grasp this basic truth sometimes try to demonstrate the divinity of Jesus like a mathematical theorem, or worse, try to "sell" Christian faith like a commercial product on the open market.

A version, says Hollander, has "limited authority"; it may even be garbled! A translation, by contrast, has, or ought to have, *total authority*, the same as that of the original literary works themselves (231). Thus we speak of the (definitive) translation of some work. In fact, all such translations date, while the original works remain. It is relevant here that Jesus has total authority (*exousia*), uniquenss, and integrity. He is not a *version* of God; he is God in the flesh. Nor is he a *paraphrase* of the deity! Such an opinion would correspond to the Docetist heresy, for which Jesus was not truly man, but simply God masquerading as a man.[5]

The original works themselves, notes Hollander, are in fact intensely committed to some sort of bias that only the information and judgment of history can illuminate (231). Here again, there is a correspondence with the Judeo-Christian revelation. By taking to himself the name of Yahweh before ever he took human flesh in Jesus, God the Creator has committed himself very deeply, with an "intense and unquestioned" commitment to a form of bias that is shocking to the rational Western mind. However

---

5. Note that translation Christology leaves room for dialogue with other world religions that claim to have incarnations or manifestations of the divinity. See too Macquarrie, *Jesus Christ*, 415–22.

much we insist that every revelation of God is also a true discovery of human religious genius and vice versa, we are left with the fact, undeniable for Christians, that God is Yahweh and Yahweh is God, the Father of Our Lord Jesus Christ. The "information and judgment of history" confront modern man with the stark fact that Yahweh has not always been good-mannered. But that is another problem.

Finally, I should note the requirements that Douglas Knight has for the translator himself: he should be an artist, a scholar, and a linguist, an expert in his field; he should have a general education, so that he can speak to the unspecialized reader; and he should be a member of his own world, "engaging it at some point, not from the sanctuary of his scholarly work but from the immediate occasions of his own life in his own time" (197). This last point reminds us how Jesus, by his conduct and his preaching, especially the parables, showed himself completely and instantly in touch with the human life of his time in all its aspects. It shows him to be the perfect translator mentioned in John 1:18.

The last and most significant aspect of translation that I wish to consider is *religious* translation, in particular the translation of the Bible. A few general principles are given by Eugene A. Nida in an article entitled "Principles of Translation as Exemplified by Bible Translating" (11–31). The difficulty of translation arises from the fact that "no two languages exhibit identical systems of organizing symbols into meaningful expressions" (13). Every message belongs to a cultural context; the problem is to reconstruct the communicative process. An example is provided by the equivalence of "kingdom of God" in Luke, written for Greco-Roman readers, and "kingdom of heaven" in Matthew, addressed to a Jewish audience, who substituted words like "heaven" and "power" for "Yahweh" and by extension for other names of God (15–16).

Lack of correspondence between English and Greek words is illustrated by our use of "love" to translate some aspects of *agapao*, *phileo*, *stergo*, and *erao*, while these words can sometimes be translated "like," "appreciate the value of," and so on. Again, the word *logos*, extremely relevant to the incarnation, is usually translated "word," but it has more than seventy meanings in Liddell and Scott, and still others in the Bible. But the Greek *epos* and *rhema* can also mean "word" (17).

Nida defines "translating" as "producing in the receptor language the closest natural equivalent to the message of the source language, first in meaning and secondly in style" (19). The emphasis on "message" is appropriate to Bible translation. One of the biggest problems is that word class structures vary. The Indo-European division of words into "object" (noun-like) words and "event" (verb-like) words is not neatly preserved in some other languages, like the Mayan languages or Tarahumara (21). There is a well-documented tendency in the Fourth Gospel to treat deed and word as one thing. This is relevant to my problem, because in God deed and essence are one; God reveals himself as at once the "wholly other" ("I am what I am") and the God active in history ("I shall be what I shall be") and possibly also as the God who supremely is ("I am that I am"). The name *Yahweh* seems designed to conceal God as much as to reveal him!

A point of some interest is the poverty of the receptor language. For example, "white as snow" may have to be translated "white as egret feathers" or simply "very, very white." Words like "Pharisees" or "Sadducees" may have to be translated by descriptive phrases (29–30). The total absence of an equivalent in the receptor language can usually be overcome by the use of neologisms, descriptive phrases, and circumlocutions. This again is very relevant, because all our talk of God is descriptive and circumlocutory, on account of the divine simplicity and inscrutability. What is particularly interesting in the Gospels is how ordinary phrases like *Ego eimi*, "I am," can assume unique and unparalleled meaning (especially John 8:58).

There is a special significance in the translation of the Bible from Hebrew into Greek and Latin, especially in the Septuagint Greek translation (LXX), one of the earliest works of literary translation.

The importance of this event is described in an article on which I shall rely for much of what follows:

> The diffusion of the Bible in the Greco-Roman world marks an epoch in the history of human relations. Perhaps for the first time, a people opened its spiritual treasures and expressed them in terms born in a quite different type of civilization. If others had already transmitted isolated stories or myths, it was in the form of adaptation, without the concern for fidelity to a sacred text; the Jewish community of Alexandria was in a sense *creating* the literary category of translation.[6]

---

6. Gribomont and Thibaut, *Richesses*, 51–105. The quotation above is from pages 51–52 (my emphasis). For the rest of this chapter, page references in my text are to this work; the translations are my own.

The task of these translators was an enormous one. "When one language stands in the historic extension of another (Latin–French) or, better still, when two languages share an almost homogeneous cultural domain (French–English), their terms can be close enough for proper equivalents to be found" (52). But it was quite otherwise with Hebrew and Greek. "The Hebrew people had lived in an exotic world whose natural conditions, industry, and institutions had no precise equivalent in Greece; to say nothing of the religious culture, which alone would have sufficed to isolate Israel. The revelation of the personal God, active in history, had produced an absolutely unique experience of pure and transcendent religion. None of the terms adopted by the Greek Bible were ready to express that religion; they underwent a shock, in their entirety, and were collectively transported into a new setting" (52).

Our authors note that the Greek is much richer in syntax and in the complexity of its parts of speech. These reflect the analytic intelligence proper to logic and philosophy. But this very richness was a defect when it came to translating the simple but pregnant concepts of the Hebrew religion. "Thanks to the structure of the semitic languages, derived parts of speech remain attached to their parent stems and grouped into families; each word continues to call forth the lowly concrete sense from which it drew its origin" (54). So the ancient translations mostly followed the Hebrew with a blind literalism, and shaped a new Greek in the process.

The authors defend the originality of the Greek Psalter in particular. They claim that "it has created means of religious expression which are superior to those of classical Greek and of the *koine* and even to those of Biblical Hebrew" (59). These authors see the Greco-Latin Psalter as showing an evolution toward the New Testament: it is written in a new language, expressing the newness of the spiritual experience lived by the community. For these authors, the Greco-Latin Psalter passes beyond the religious level of the Hebrew (89).

Examples of the evolution of religious thought are cited from the versions of Psalm 21, verses 1–7. The name Yahweh has been suppressed in favor of *Kurios* (Lord) and *Dominus*. This was done out of respect; it is suggested that the name Yahweh, as the name of the tribal God of the Hebrew people, was found to be archaic and particular.[7] C. H. Dodd suggested that "by merely eliminating the name of God, the LXX contributed

---

7. Ernest Renan, the complete rationalist, found the name Yahweh decidedly inferior. *Life of Jesus*, 63, note 28.

to the definition of monotheism."[8] At the same time, the word *Kurios* was expanded in meaning by being adopted for God. "In entering into the Bible, *Kurios* acquired a sense at once personal and absolute, taking on the unique and transcendent character of the God of the Covenant" (64).

The history of the word *Sabaoth* provides an interesting example of religious translation. The expression "Yahweh Sabaoth" has been translated "Lord God of hosts," referring to heavenly hosts, and not just to Israel's armies. Sabaoth includes supernatural powers as well as human forces . . . all the power that Yahweh put at the service of his people in their battles. For the Hebrews, the supernatural powers were manifested by cosmic phenomena. The Greek words *dunameis* (for powers) and *pantokrator* (for God the Almighty) are attempts to translate this idea. In Latin we find the versions *Dominus omnipotens* (almighty Lord); *Dominus Sabaoth*, a transliteration that occurred in the Tridentine Mass; *Dominus virtutum*, open to the suggestion of supernatural powers; and, in St. Jerome, *Dominus exercituum* (Lord of armies), a somewhat restrictive and "rationalist" rendering. The English "Lord God of hosts" is suitably archaic and avoids a restriction to earthly armies. The translation of divine attributes often shows development and fusion of concepts. The *sweetness* of God (for his *goodness*) gives a warmer, more personal note and is closely linked to religious experience: "Taste and see that the Lord is sweet." The *mercy* of God is a complex notion associated with love and compassion. The *anger* (or wrath) of God assumed a central place in Jewish piety at a late date, with more attention paid to the religious nature of sin than to its moral consequences. The concept of hope (*elpis*) is developed in the Greek Psalter to imply assured confidence in the intervention of God, confident prayer, and the desire for divine grace, succor, support, and intervention (82).

Because the Septuagint is so faithful, word for word, to its original, words like *kardia* (heart) take on the meaning of the Hebrew *leb*. So the new language is itself modified to assume the meanings of the old. Our authors note that neither the Jews nor the primitive church wrote to satisfy a literary elite. The humble faithful did not follow Attic usage. *Koine* Greek and vulgar Latin provided a medium in which the verbal imagery of the Hebrew could be preserved.

---

8. *The Bible and the Greeks* (London, 1935) 4; cited in *On Translaion*, 63, note 29.

We see here in passing the opposition between religion and culture, comparable to the opposition in modern times between religion and technology, which causes so many religious believers to wonder at God's providential plan for the human race. That the opposition between religion and culture is a superficial one can be glimpsed from the great religious art and music of the past, and from the fine flowering of both religion and culture in a man like the late Monsignor Ronald Knox.

In conclusion, our authors acknowledge that a humanist formation is said to be a bad preparation for using the old Psalters. They suggest that the humanist ideal should be enlarged, and that universities need to look again at Christian literature, at the masterpieces that have had the deepest spiritual influence on Western culture (105). One may remark, a little cynically perhaps, that the inevitable process of "debunking" the classics will doubtless bring this about in due course!

The application of this wealth of material to the incarnation is surely obvious. The process of divine revelation takes its origin in a primitive Jewish tribe. The rich, simple vigor of Hebrew religious thought has to be translated into the great humanist languages of the world, thereby elevating these languages in the religious sense, and at the same time abstracting the religious attitudes that were common, at root, to the primitive metaphors.

Likewise, God became man at an epoch of relative simplicity, when the clear-cut ideas needed to translate divinity into human form were common tender. But every age needs to grasp the incarnation for itself; in any age the terms are not lacking to make the simple but profound truth of God in the flesh come alive in the language and culture of the time.

But I must look next at the radical possibility of the incarnation before moving on to consider its radical impossibility. I now ask, what is the basis in human nature for God to be able to translate his Word into human flesh and form?

9

Finitum Capax Infiniti (Martin Luther)
Man as God's Image

The title of this chapter contains a Latin phrase meaning "the finite is capable of the infinite." This implies that God has a way of bestowing himself on man, even though man is finite and God is infinite. According to the late supervisor of my PhD thesis, Professor E. L. Mascall of King's College London, this phrase was used in that sense by Martin Luther. A contrary phrase was attributed to John Calvin, as the title of the next chapter indicates. These phrases give an ecumenical flavor to my thesis, so I am happy to use them here.

In trying to examine the possibility that God can translate his Word into human form, we are like a student of astronomy who studies the heavens by looking through the wrong end of a telescope. However, even this analogy is generous to our understanding of God. The possibilities of knowing God are God's, and his knowledge of his possibilities is infinite and exhaustive. God fully understands himself and all that it is possible for him to do. Further, no created intellect can have this total comprehension, not even the human intellect of Jesus himself. That is why, at the height of neoscholastic triumphalism, the Holy Office simply claimed that Jesus knew in his human mind all the things that God actually does create, not all the things that God could possibly create.

But we, mortals that we are, do not understand these possibilities; we have to argue from what is the case to what can be the case. Failure to grasp this fact has led many people into atheism, and others into an infantile form of theism that affirms belief in a magical God—a God whom a rational, adult human being must classify as a criminal lunatic. For if

God were magic, and if all magical possibilities were open to his omnipotence, he would have to be the perfect sadist in order to create a world like this one. I do not believe in such a God and I feel that we must, with St. Thomas Aquinas, hold fast to the fact that God cannot do the impossible, and hold just as fast to the further fact that, apart from simple "nonsense" concepts like "square circle," we have very little idea of what things are impossible. The Lucan passage, "No word (*rhema*) will be impossible with God" (Luke 1:37) can in fact be applied in this sense because we do not know precisely what concepts are indeed "words" (i.e., possible things).[1]

A more subtle example of a nonsense concept (other than the obvious one of "square circle") is provided by Bertrand Russell's famous paradox about "the set of all those sets which are not members of themselves," which proved so devastating to the formalists. Only when we ask, "Is this set a member of itself?" do we see that its concept is self-contradictory and absurd. The nonmathematician may prefer to think about the village barber who shaves all and only those men in the village who do not shave themselves. The interesting question is, does he shave himself?

Of course this is not to deny that we have knowledge of first principles, such as that the whole is greater than the part, or that an absolute beginning is impossible. But we are in constant danger of trying to push the limits of this *a priori* knowledge beyond just bounds; that is why a critical philosophy like logical positivism is such a boon. This sort of philosophy will, it seems to me, ultimately prove to be the best ally of sound theism, because it will destroy the basis of atheism along with naive theism.

The possibility for God to translate his Word into human form is guaranteed to us by the biblical teaching that man is made in God's image. This is made clear by the priestly writer of the first chapter of Genesis: "God created man in the image of himself, in the image of God he created him, male and female he created them" (Gen 1:27).

This poem can be clarified by referring to the preceding verse: "God said, 'Let us make man in our own image, in the likeness of ourselves, and let them be masters of the fish of the sea, the birds of heaven, the cattle, all the wild beasts and all the reptiles that crawl upon the earth'" (Gen 1: 26).

Eugene H. Maly commented, "*Selem* (image) means, ordinarily, an exact copy or reproduction . . . [T]he harshness of the implication [of anthropomorphism] is softened by the addition of *demut* (likeness),

---

1. In its biblical setting, the passage would seem to mean rather that God can do anything that he promises to do, (Gen 18:14).

ordinarily meaning resemblance or similarity. The Semites knew of no dichotomy in man in our terms; the whole man, as a complete personality, had God's image, manifested especially in the resulting ability to rule over other creatures . . . Man, as God's image, is his representative on earth (statues represented the ancient kings in those regions of the empire where they could not be present personally)."[2]

Theologians like St. Augustine saw the image of God in man's "soul," that is, his rational part, and the likeness in his body or "inferior" part. It is worth noting that man, by his intellect and will, is able to say "I love you" to God, and in so doing enter into a personal relationship with him. Whether the beasts in their own way can say "I love you" to God is another question. The Yahwist author of the second chapter of Genesis shows man naming the beasts, and so exercising dominion over them; he adds that "no helpmate suitable for man was found for him" among the beasts (Gen 2:20; cf. also Gen 1:28).

Prescinding from neo-Platonic dualism, whether it be true or false, the life of intelligence and will allows man to exercise a godlike dominion over the world. The life of knowledge and love enables man to know truth and to pursue goodness; it allows for the contemplation of wisdom, the greatest of God's gifts (Wisdom 7:7–14). But it is in man's dominion over the world that the Hebrews saw the divine image most clearly:

> Yet you have made him [man] little less than a god,
> you have crowned him with glory and splendor,
> made him lord over the work of your hands,
> set all things under his feet.
> (Ps 8:5–6)

(See, too, 1 Cor 15:26, where these last words are applied to Christ. Note that in the next chapter of this book I shall develop the theme that Jesus exercised this dominion as God walking on earth in human form, paradoxically showing his lordship by becoming the servant of all.)

The other part of the message of Genesis is that man is created in God's image as male and female (Gen 1:27). This fact has created difficulty for some theologians with their Christology, because Jesus was undoubtedly male, and celibate as well.[3] Karl Barth tried to resolve the

---

2. JBC 2:20.

3. The celibacy of Jesus can hardly be questioned on historical grounds (see, for example, Meier, *A Marginal Jew*, vol. 1, 332–450); to question it on theological grounds

difficulty by considering the relationship of Christ as masculine and the church as feminine. But this was a rather forced notion, and I think that Barth's failure to appreciate Catholic Mariology let him down here.[4]

The subject of Mariology is highly charged with emotion and needs a treatise to itself. More precisely, Mary deserves every tribute that we can honestly pay her. To date, the main trouble with Mariology is that it has been bedeviled by controversy, especially Catholic-Protestant controversy. After a Protestant says, "Catholics worship Mary!" and a Catholic replies, "Catholics adore God alone, and venerate Mary and the Saints!" that is often considered to be the end of the matter. But it is in fact not even the beginning.

The role of Mary in Catholic psychology, setting aside the dogmatic formulas, is that she takes the place of the feminine principle in the deity, which has been suppressed for historical and anthropological reasons. The words *Father* and *Son* have obvious and necessary historical connotations. But if we were making up a theology in a vacuum, supposing such a theology could ever be meaningful to historically conditioned human beings, we might want to replace *Father* with a word that is positively neuter, combining all that is positive in *Father* and *Mother*; similarly for *Son*, with *Daughter* serving instead of *Mother*. To exclude these male dominated terms from the deity, which is neither male nor female, would be an enormous exercise and, as my next paragraph shows, would be useless anyway.

It takes very little imagination to see that such a theology would be so abstract as to be virtually meaningless. For one thing, God the Son is forever revealed to us in Jesus and is inseparably united by a hypostatic union to the sacred humanity of Jesus. Even the most ardent feminist would have some difficulty in getting round that fact. So, in fact, whether we like it or not, Mary has taken the place, in God's theology if not in ours, of the feminine principle in the deity. This was seen by the Swiss psychologist Carl Jung, himself a (liberal) Protestant, who found it one of

---

would seem to be against the whole thrust of the New Testament. Cf. Matt 22:30, Mark 12:25, and especially Luke 20:34–36.

4. For Barth on Catholic Mariology, *Church Dogmatics* I/2, 139–46. It seems that Barth was very far from making a carefl study of Catholic Mariology in the official documents of the Roman Catholic Church.

Finitum Capax Infiniti (Martin Luther)

the greatest assets of the Catholic faith and even used it as a "stick" with which to beat his fellow Protestants![5]

But because I am engaged in writing Christology and not Mariology, I shall omit any further reflections on this theme.[6] Agreeing that man is in some sense God's image, we must next contend with the apparent impossibility of mapping the infinite on the finite. To this topic I now turn.

---

5. Jung, *Answer to Job* 165–78. But note that Jung's interpretation of the Assumption of Mary would hardly satisfy any Catholic who believes that Jesus himself truly rose, in his flesh and bones, from the dead; p. 170: "It does not matter at all that a physically impossible fact is asserted, because all religious assertions are physical impossibilities." But see p. 171: "Just as the person of Christ cannot be replaced by an organization, so the bride cannot be replaced by the Church. The feminine, like the masculine, demands an equally personal representation."

6. For a feminist view of Catholic Mariology, see Fiorenza, *Jesus*, chapter 6.

10

Finitum non Capax Infiniti (John Calvin)
Mapping the Infinite on the Finite

As I mentioned at the beginning of my last chapter, the supervisor of my PhD thesis, the late Professor E. L. Mascall of King's College London, mentioned two Latin phrases: one attributed to Martin Luther and the other to John Calvin. He suggested I write a chapter on each. The Latin phrase above means "The finite is not capable of the infinite," and therefore points to the impossibility of God bestowing himself on man.

On the face of it, the infinite cannot be translated into finite form. Certainly, the finite cannot contain and circumscribe the infinite. The metaphysical infinite, being infinite in act, is unique. In this it can be contrasted with the mathematical infinite.

Modern mathematicians after Cantor have had to admit the existence of orders of infinity, since there is more than one transfinite number; although the theory of transfinite numbers remains problematic and gives rise to difficult philosophical questions in the foundations of mathematics.[1]

Because the finite cannot contain and circumscribe the infinite, we have to admit a radical impossibility of the incarnation of God. The Jewish people continue to bear witness to this impossibility, but their witness is historically conditioned and has been unfortunately connected with a positive belief in the impossibility of a plurality of persons in the deity. In this belief, I think, they are untrue to their own deepest traditions. But that is another question.

---

1. Fraenkel, *Abstract Set Theory*, chapter 1; also Bell, *Men of Mathematics*, Vol. 2, 612–39.

Finitum non Capax Infiniti (John Calvin)

It will be useful here to refer to the fundamental mathematical notion of a *mapping* from one set on to another. A mapping is a pairing or relating that sets up a correspondence between the elements of one set and the elements of the other set. If the mapping is a one-to-one correspondence that preserves structure, it is called an *isomorphism*.[2] Sets that are isomorphic are not distinguished; they are regarded as being identical. So, if the infinite could be mapped on to the finite in a one-to-one way, it would be in accordance with modern scientific usage to regard the finite term as being identical with God.

If I were speaking about some order of mathematical infinity, there could be no question of mapping it on to the finite in a one-to-one way. Indeed, the existence of different orders of mathematical infinity is established precisely by showing the impossibility of setting up a one-to-one correspondence between the sets concerned. Any mapping of the mathematical infinite on to the finite would have to be many-to-one rather than one-to-one; in fact it would have to be infinitely many-to-one.[3] But I am not speaking about the mathematical infinite; I am speaking about the metaphysical infinite, or infinite in act, and, paradoxically, that makes my task easier. It is true that God's infinity contains every possible mathematical infinity in some supereminent and simple but inscrutable manner. In this sense, the infinite cannot be mapped on the finite. Indeed, God's infinity is actual, precisely in those qualities or attributes that are proper to God; in other words, God's infinity is a matter of quality and intension rather than of quantity and extension. And it is just these divine attributes that are mapped on the humanity of Jesus, as I proceed to show.

My task here is to relate the Old Testament to the New Testament, and to show that the God of Israel, Creator of the universe, has been expressed in human form in Jesus of Nazareth. Because I am a finite being, I am not fully equipped for this task. Indeed, none of us are so equipped.

---

2. A correspondence between two sets is one-to-one if to each element of the first set there corresponds exactly one element of the second set and vice versa. The preservation of structure means the invariance under the mapping of any mathematical operations defined on the respective sets. Isomorphism is usually defined between groups. Patterson, *Topology*, 81.

3. An example can be constructed by mapping the real numbers between 0 and 1 (which are infinitely many, with cardinal number c) on to the ten integers 0, 1, 2, . . . , 9 by associating each number, written in (unambiguous) decimal form, with the integer represented by its first digit.

It is my hope to suggest lines of thought that scholars more learned than I can follow in order to draw their own conclusions.

Because I am a Roman Catholic, I begin with the description of God given by the First Vatican Council in chapter 1 of the dogmatic constitution *Dei Filius*: The holy catholic apostolic Roman Church believes and confesses that there is one God, living and true, the creator and the Lord of heaven and earth, almighty, eternal, immense, incomprehensible, infinite in intellect and will and every perfection; who, since he is one singular, utterly simple and unchangeable spiritual substance, is to be proclaimed distinct from the world in reality and essence, in himself and of himself most blessed, and ineffably exalted above all things beside himself which exist or can be conceived.[4]

This is an extremely Scholastic description of God. But Scholastic descriptions of God are not as far from the Bible as some might imagine. Although the conventional textbook attributes of God are listed in *Dei Filius*, the order of these attributes is not that of a philosophical treatise. God is called one, living and true; that is, he has the distinctive characteristics of Yahweh, who admitted no rivals and no idols, who was alive and able to help Israel, and who was true and real as opposed to false and fictitious gods.

God is called creator and Lord of heaven and earth. He is thus proclaimed as the universal God, the God of all people. Then the distinctive divine attributes are listed: omnipotence, because no word is impossible with God (Gen 18:14; Luke 1:37); eternity and immensity, because God is not bounded by space and time; incomprehensibility, because no finite intellect can know him exhaustively; and infinity in intellect and will and every perfection, implying the divine life of knowledge and love and perfect bliss. Finally, God is proclaimed to be utterly simple, unchangeable, spiritual, distinct from the world, supremely happy, and supremely exalted.

Of course, this definition does not tell us the whole truth about God. For one thing, the fact that God is love is left to be inferred from the perfection of his will. God's omnipotence is put into greater prominence than his love, in accordance with the historical development of the Judeo-Christian revelation. In fact, the primacy of love is a comparatively recent insight. God is Love by name and Love by nature, and this fact is on the

---

4. *DzS* 3001 (1782); my translation.

Finitum non Capax Infiniti (John Calvin)

whole more significant than his omnipotence, which is so easily misconstrued and misunderstood.

But let us further consider the attributes that the Council stressed. In previous chapters of this book, I have shown how Jesus expresses in his human heart the love that he feels as Son for the Father, for the Holy Spirit, and for the whole of creation. It is more important now to see how Jesus can and does express the omnipotence of God, his omniscience, and even his immensity and eternity, for only thus can we discover that the infinite, precisely as infinite, has been mapped on the finite.

The most paradoxical attributes admit in fact of very simple expression. The *eternity* of God means that God exists, but not in time. This is all but impossible for us to comprehend: We can conceive eternity only as an instant that spans all of time and all possible time, but we cannot truly comprehend successive duration.[5] And so we must resort to metaphor. Boethius, when languishing in prison, produced the perfect human definition of eternity: "*interminabilis vitae tota simul et perfecta possessio*": the possession, all at once and perfectly, of boundless life. By contrast, St. Augustine described eternity's duration in terms of knowledge: God's knowledge is morning knowledge, while ours is evening knowledge. Eternity itself, however, is most starkly expressed in a single polemical utterance:

> I tell you most solemnly
> before Abraham ever was
> I Am.
> (John 8:58)[6]

The *immensity* of God means that God exists, but this existence is without spatial restriction. God is not in a place; he is not absorbed by any place, or by the set of all possible places. Yet he is present to every place, and his presence is his essence and his power. As St. Thomas Aquinas said, place cannot exist unless being exists, and wherever there is being,

---

5. The humanity of Jesus, the expression of eternity in human form, began existence in a finite point in time. The Johannine sentence, "Now, Father, it is time for you to glorify me with that glory I had with you before ever the world was" (John 17:5) could refer to the predestination of Jesus.

6. Such Johannine phrases may belong to the author rather than to Jesus. But note too that the Greek *ego eimi* contained in this phrase occurs in the Synoptic Gospels (e.g., Mark 6:50) as well as in John and may echo the name of God, JHWH, from the Old Testament.

there is God. It is inconceivable that Christ's sacred humanity should transcend space or exist in every place, although Martin Luther did not think so. But the Johannine Christ reveals, in one pregnant sentence, his divine ubiquity when he says to Nathanael, "Before Philip came to call you, I saw you under the fig tree" (John 1: 48).[7]

The *simplicity* of God means that he is without parts, physical or metaphysical. He has no body; in him essence and existence are one. All his thoughts are one thought in him, identical with himself and with his love. The divine simplicity is expressed in Jesus by his complete single-mindedness, which he both practices and preaches.

The Sermon on the Mount shocks by its single-mindedness, irreducible to a legal system: "No one can be the slave of two masters: he will either hate the first and love the second, or treat the first with respect and the second with scorn. You cannot be the slave both of God and of money" (Matt 6:24).

It is the same before Caiaphas and before Pilate: "You will see the Son of Man seated at the right hand of the Power and coming with the clouds of heaven" (Mark 14:62); "I came into the world for this: to bear witness to the truth." (John 18:37). God did not reveal himself to men by means of carefully qualified statements.

The *omnipotence* of God is revealed to us in Jesus mainly by way of his miracles. These recorded miracles must give twenty-first century man food for thought; for, as Rudolf Bultmann has repeatedly assured us, modern man does not believe in miracles.[8]

This raises a very complex issue; I shall just make a few remarks here. Of course, there is no extrinsic criterion for discarding the miracles of Jesus from the Gospel story and retaining anything else. On the other hand, the intrinsic argument against miracle is a very powerful one. It is not based on an *a priori* principle, as some religious apologists suppose. Even the arch-rationalist Ernest Renan did not assert that miracles are impossible. The argument against miracle is based on the fact that, for most of us, the totality of our direct experience of life is completely consistent with the possibility that miracles in fact never happen. This is a very powerful dissuasive, not to be easily shrugged off in the name of religious propaganda, for it involves the question of intellectual honesty,

---

7. See note 6, above.

8. Bultmann, *Jesus Christ and Mythology* 37–38. For a modern Catholic view of the gospel miracles, see Senior, *NJBC*, 81:89–117; Meier, *Marginal Jew*, vol. 2, 509–1038.

Finitum non Capax Infiniti (John Calvin)

understood as the obedience of the mind to reality as opposed to wishful thinking. My own position on the miracles of Jesus is that I am inclined to treat the gospel story with respect as containing the story of our redemption; but I do not feel constrained to believe in any particular miracle as a matter of divine faith (this would be to make one of the aids to faith into the object of faith and even a possible obstacle to faith, like using a crutch as a lethal weapon!); at the same time, I utterly reject any magical explanation of miracle, just as I have rejected a magical explanation of divine omnipotence.

At this point I really should try to define my use of the word "magic." A magical trick done on a stage has an explanation; we know this, even though we do not know what the explanation is. By "magic" I mean something that has absolutely no explanation even in principle: all one can say is, "God has acted here, *Digitus Dei est hic*." My objection to magic of this sort is the one already stated: if God were magic in this sense, he would be a perfect sadist to create a world like this one.

Rejecting any magical explanation both of omnipotence and of miracle, I can accept the miracles of Jesus as the translation of God's omnipotence into human form.[9] Here the *nature miracles* take pride of place, because they show that complete command over the forces of nature which belongs to the Creator alone. Not even a theory of Jesus as God's plenipotentiary can account for the manner in which these miracles are worked. Jesus rebukes the wind and says to the sea, "Quiet now! Be calm!" The wind drops, and all is calm again (Mark 4:39). The walking on the sea is a sign of complete independence and self-sufficiency (Mark 6:45–56); in Matthew, Jesus shows himself able to sustain Peter in this feat as well (Matt 14:22–36). The multiplication of the loaves recalls God's power to feed his people in the desert (Mark 6:33–44; 8:1–9; cf. John 6:30–31).

To modern man the *healing miracles* are more effective signs of *divine* power; for modern man tends to think of omnipotence in terms of love rather than of magic. The healing done by Jesus is mostly effected by a simple word, sometimes at a distance, and sometimes with physical touching, or after prayer. There is an interesting contrast between the raising of the widow's son to life by Elijah at Zarephath and the raising of the widow's son at Nain by Jesus. Elijah prayed, "Yahweh my God, may

---

9. I am also not concerned to offer an "anti-magical" explanation of miracle, e.g., faith-healing, both because it might be wrong and because it would give offence without just cause.

the soul of this child, I beg you, come into him again!" (1 Kings 17:21). By contrast, Jesus said, "Young man, I tell you to get up" (Luke: 7:14), which indicates that the divine power over life and death was his without the asking.

Omniscience is a divine attribute that has been attributed to Jesus' humanity in a literal and mechanical way by the Scholastics and the Holy Office. But here again, the truth is probably more subtle. Once again, there is the question of metaphysical possibilities and impossibilities. For example, there is no evidence that any man born in Jesus' time, divine or not, could have known of the theories of Einstein. "Infused" knowledge does not solve this *impasse*; the evidence suggests that "infused" knowledge is of a sapiential, charismatic order, rather than of a scientific, conceptual order. But divine omniscience is expressed in Jesus' astonishing authority and wisdom, in his complete command of every debating situation, above all by his perfectly simple and direct insight into the secrets of God's inner life, the life of the Trinity, so that his exposition of these secrets left the disciples with the knowledge that they had glimpsed the divine reality itself (John 17:29–30).

I have said that, for the Jews, man is made in God's image because of man's godlike dominance over the world. Now Jesus rules by becoming the servant; in him, God assumes the lowliness of man, and man is thereby raised to the dignity of God. Jesus is at the service of others by his tireless ministry of teaching and healing. When John the Baptist is killed and Jesus would like to be alone, he yields to his pity for the people's needs (Matt 14:14).

In one respect Jesus appears to dominate in a most frightening manner. By this I mean his exercise of judgment and the threat of judgment. There are the woes against the scribes and Pharisees, especially in Matthew, chapter 23. These should be read in the light of Jesus' lament over Jerusalem: "How often have I longed to gather your children, as a hen gathers her chicks under her wings, and you refused" (Matt 23:37).[10]

Again, there is the threat of eternal fire and of the worm that does not die, and the repeated references to weeping and gnashing of teeth, which so upset Bertrand Russell.[11] I content myself with the understand-

---

10. But some modern biblical scholars think that the woes in Matthew, chapter 23, reflect the polemic of the early church against the synagogue. See for example Meier, *Marginal Jew*, vol. 2, 353; Lüdemann, *Great Deception*, 25–29.

11. Russell, *Why I am not a Christian*, 13.

Finitum non Capax Infiniti (John Calvin)

ing that the gospel is a challenge to moral seriousness, a call to action, not an attempt to induce a neurotic and paralyzing fear.

The parables of Dives and Lazarus, and of the sheep and the goats, set this teaching in perspective. So does the incident of the woman taken in adultery, with its emphasis on forgiveness and amendment. Finally, the word "friend" addressed to Judas at the moment of betrayal prevents us from reaching any facile conclusions about reprobation.[12] The point here is that the judgments which Jesus utters against the Pharisees are both human and divine. They are human judgments made by the rejected prophet, at a particular point of space and time. They also express the divine judgment on all human legal systems and on all human righteousness. To press them beyond that, as Christians have done in the past, is both mistaken and shameful. The judgments expressing approval and reprobation, as in the parable of the sheep and the goats, are human expressions of the judgment of God. These expressed judgments, our human thoughts about God, pronounce finally and irrevocably, in perfect accord with the requirements of infinite mercy and infinite justice, attributes that are not distinct in God himself.

I have expressed, in summary form, something of what I think it means for God to translate his Word into human form, to map the infinite on the finite in a strictly one-to-one way. I conclude this chapter by saying that the Godhead can be described by the two qualities of omnipotence and love. If God is not omnipotent, then he is not God and is of no use to man. If God does not love us, then the human joke is too obscene to be even tragic; tragedy requires a certain measure of dignity.

The argument for atheism from the existence of evil says that, if God were omnipotent, God could prevent evil; and, if God were loving, God would prevent it. St. Augustine, like a good Roman, accepted God's omnipotence as axiomatic. He tried to define God's love in such a way as to make it consistent with a "magical" omnipotence: for St. Augustine, God would not have allowed evil in his universe unless he could draw greater good from it.

It is no fault of St. Augustine's that I find his God to be a criminal lunatic, not only very wicked, but extremely silly as well. Because of his magical concept of omnipotence, St. Augustine could not believe in any

---

12. Honesty compels me to state my personal opinion that hell is empty. But see Matthew 7:13-14; Luke 13:23-24. Note, too, that the promise of resurrection in John 11:25-26 is attached to faith; cf., too, John 6:55.

other sort of God. For me, God's love is axiomatic: God is Love by name and Love by nature. We do not know the "limits" of omnipotence, because we do not know just what is metaphysically possible and what is not.

But I believe that God's plan is one of perfect reconciliation, because no lesser plan is worthy of God's love or indeed of God's power; and that perfect reconciliation may require extreme polarization, not because God is a crazy fiend, but because that is the way things are. In the modern idiom, that is "how it is." In the idiom of St. Thomas Aquinas, the divine will follows the divine intellect, which reads the possibilities of things in the divine essence.

For this reason I find the image of God in Jesus because he loved us unto death. The miracles of Jesus show that he could do the things that only God can do. But his concern for others shows that he could love as only God can love. This is summed up in St. Luke's story about the widow of Nain. "When the Lord saw her he felt sorry for her. 'Do not cry,' he said" (Luke 7:13). There is no request for a miracle, no demand for faith. He felt sorry for her; that is all. Jesus does not work the miracle in order to prove his divinity; he works the miracle out of divine pity. And here there is proof enough.

This concludes my study of the technical aspects of translation Christology. It remains to consider the more specifically religious aspect of translation Christology, which is the actual revelation of God by, in, and through Jesus Christ.

11

Religious Aspects of Translation Christology

The *possibility* of the incarnation is its least interesting aspect; its *reality* is the truth by which we live. This reality is the knowledge of God revealed in Jesus Christ: "Eternal life is this: to know you, the only true God, and Jesus Christ whom you have sent" (John 17:3).

According to translation Christology, Jesus Christ in the incarnation appears as translator and translated; he translates the Father's Godhead for us, and he is himself the Son translated into human form. We need then to look at God revealed by Jesus Christ, and at God revealed in Jesus Christ; we need to consider the reality of Father and Son as translated for us by the Christ event.

But the Christ event is not yet completed; or, if it is completed, it is not yet fulfilled. The continuing revelation of God that is also the articulation and clarification of God's final revelation in Jesus Christ is brought about by the action of the Holy Spirit. But in fulfilling his task of revelation (John 16:13), the Spirit also reveals himself. As such, we must therefore consider how the Spirit completes the work of translation by helping us to understand the work already completed in Jesus Christ.

12

God Revealed by Jesus Christ
The Eternal Father

The revelation of God by Jesus Christ is the climax of God's self-disclosure. It is final, in relation to what went before: "At various times in the past and in various different ways God spoke to our ancestors through the prophets; but in our own time, the last days, he has spoken to us through his Son, the Son that he has appointed to inherit everything and through whom he has made everything there is" (Heb 1:1–2). It is also a definitive revelation, in relation to what comes afterwards: "For the foundation, nobody can lay any other than the one which has already been laid, that is Jesus Christ" (1 Cor 3:11); "For, of all the names in the world given to men, this is the only one by which we can be saved" (Acts 4:12).

In preceding chapters I have shown how the concept of a definitive or authoritative translation throws light on the uniqueness of Jesus. We must now consider the uniqueness and normative character of the revelation of God that Jesus brought. As already noted, in order for humans to find meaning in the revelation brought by Jesus Christ, humans had to already have some experience of God. At the same time, the revelation elevated, enlightened, and enriched all previous knowledge of God, much in the same way that the translation of the Bible into Greek elevated and enriched the Greek language. Instead of trying in vain to match the Hebrew Bible by finding an exact shade of meaning in existent Greek, the Septuagint translators put down simple Greek equivalents of Hebrew terms, and so invested each of these simple Greek words with a new religious sense.

As God prepared the Greek world and the Greek language to receive the Hebrew Bible, so he prepared the Jewish people and the Jewish religion to receive the message of Jesus. The preparation was more intense, and is rightly called supernatural because it occurred as a personal revelation brought about through biblical and prophetic inspiration. We must look more closely at the revelation of God in the Old Testament in order to see how this same God was preparing to declare himself definitively as the Father of our Lord Jesus Christ.

Before considering God's revelation of himself in Judaism, I must say a word about natural theology. I would insist that the only reality that ever could exist is the triune God and what he should choose to create; thus the division of theology into natural (non-Trinitarian) and supernatural (Trinitarian) is somewhat artificial. Likewise, I would insist that stories of a fall of man, as we have received them, are mythological and that they need a great deal more demythologizing than they have yet received from traditionalist Scripture scholars. I hold this to be true of the Genesis story along with the others. (I suspect that many scholars are held in check by conservative church authorities.) Therefore, other than from revelation, an abstract consideration of what man's reason could tell him is groundless; indeed, a careful historical study of what man actually knew without revelation, not forgetting St. Paul's distinction between what man actually did know and what he should have known (Rom 1:20), is required. Pending such a study, I can see no real difference between a sound natural theology and what Karl Barth called "general revelation." The practical point would seem to be that God inhabits the praises of Israel (Ps 22:3); and Christians who find God in the mountains and the rivers, in the sea and the sky, might reflect that they are able to do so only because the Psalmist did so before them (e.g., Pss 104, 108; 93, 95; 8; 29).

The God of Old Testament revelation is primarily personal.[1] This is to say, he is someone who enters into relationships with his people and with the world that he has created. He is a God who takes the initiative, a God who is active in history. Indeed he is the God of history, the one and only God who is really there. All other gods are figments of peoples' imaginations. St. Paul will mitigate the severity of this attitude by telling the men of Athens that the God whom they worship unknown is in fact the true God who made the world (Acts 17:23–24).

---

1. For a biblical treatment of the God of Israel, see McKenzie, "Aspects," 77.

The God of the Bible has many names: Elohim, Shaddai, Adonai, and especially Yahweh. As Yahweh, he revealed himself to Moses and led the Israelites out of Egypt, laying the foundation of the special relationship that the primitive history of the Bible traces back to Abraham and even to Noah. As nomadic people, the Israelites worshipped the God of their Fathers, the God of Abraham, of Isaac, and of Jacob.

This God was to some extent a tribal God, but he is unique in the sense that there is no other like him: there is no other god like God, no other elohim like Yahweh. Israel was forbidden to worship any other God; wherever man and nature are found, Yahweh's writ runs. All images of Yahweh are forbidden to the Israelites because Yahweh is unlike anything in the visible universe.

God is constantly described in anthropomorphic terms. This is so throughout the Old Testament, and it will appear below in the passages I cite from Jeremiah (31:3) and Hosea (2:21–22) about God's love for Israel as his bride. In this way his personal nature is maintained in fact and not just in theory. He responds to love or to disobedience with a personal response of love or anger. His relation to Israel is described as that of father to son, husband to wife (cf. Ps 2:7–8 and references above). His saving acts arise from personal benevolence; the law is an expression of his personal will. The masculine image, historically inevitable, is balanced by one eloquent passage:

> Does a woman forget her baby at the breast,
> or fail to cherish the son of her womb?
> Yet even if these forget,
> I will never forget you.
> (Isa 49:15)

In the Old Testament (and indeed in the New Testament) God is often described in terms of myth. In contrast with discursive reasoning, myth clothes its statements about ultimate realities in images that cannot correspond to literal truth. A simple example of myth is in the statement, "He [Jesus] ascended into heaven." (Acts 1:9 actually says: "He was lifted up while they looked on, and a cloud took him from their sight.") The concept "ascended" reveals the mythical nature of the statement. But the statement says something about the exaltation of Jesus, about his personal victory over sin and death, which is the pledge of final victory for the kingdom or reign of God. So it is an example by metaphor.

God Revealed by Jesus Christ

Thus the creation myth of Genesis uses the image of God's effective words, such as "Let there be light" (Gen 1:3), to show the effortless supremacy of the creative deity. Mesopotamian mythopoeic thought appears to be modified in the Bible by the character of Yahweh. Thus, the element of struggle is eliminated from the story of creation; in the story of the deluge, capricious anger becomes righteous indignation at the wickedness of men.

God's interest in his creation and his concern with it did not end after the six days of genesis (Genesis, chapter one). Yahweh sustains and defends the material universe against the forces of disintegration. But these forces have no power to match that of Yahweh, so dualism and cyclic conflict are avoided.

Yahweh makes dawn and darkness (Amos 4:13; 5:3), measures the waters in the hollow of his hand (Isa 40:12), gives breath and spirit to those who walk the earth (Isa 42:5). The creative acts of Psalm 104 recur each day.[2]

The dealings of Yahweh with man through nature are not capricious, but are measured by his wisdom. When nature strikes man with disaster, it is seen as the weapon of Yahweh's anger. Sin has cosmic repercussions because Yahweh withholds his blessings and then uses nature as the executor of his judgments. Yet all the phenomena of nature and all its events are integrated into Yahweh's saving will.

The character of God appears most clearly in the Old Testament in his relation with Israel, his covenanted people. The analogy of covenant is now usually taken as basic for God's relationship to Israel. Israel is the people of God, chosen for service, not for privilege; its only privilege is to bear on its shoulders the burden of the world's sin, the responsibility for the world's salvation (cf. John 4:22: "salvation comes from the Jews").

Man in the Old Testament is not an incarnate spirit but an animated body. The community has a corporate personality, represented in retrospect by the patriarch and later by the king. Yahweh enters into relationship with this community (Israel) by a series of positive personal actions, culminating in a number of covenants. The relationship that arises in this way is variously described: Yahweh is a father and Israel is his son; Yahweh "begets" Israel by forming a people for himself. The resulting relationship is one of love, devotion, and obedience.

---

2. Psalm 77:55; Psalm 2: 7, 8.

Again, Yahweh is a husband and Israel is his bride. Here again the initiative is with Yahweh, according to the pattern of ancient marriage. But the relationship is more clearly seen to be one of total, mutual, exclusive love; Yahweh can be demanding and even jealous. The fidelity of Israel is a work of love, and the infidelity of Israel is a personal offence against Yahweh.

Yahweh is a devoted shepherd, and Israel is his flock, confidently relying on his protection. Yahweh is also the kinsman or "avenger" (or "redeemer") of Israel. He undertakes this role freely, not through ties of blood. Yahweh is king and Israel is his subject, as the title "Lord" implies.

The covenant theme means that Yahweh has freely chosen Israel as his people, out of love. He made them a people by delivering them from Egypt and by giving them the land of Canaan. His election of Israel imposes on Israel the responsibility of recognizing Yahweh alone as God, and of keeping his commandments. So Israel is chosen for responsibility and obligation, not merely for privilege.

Here one must note the tension between divine revelation and human discovery. The gift of the land of Canaan to Israel was brought about by means that few people living today, whether Christians, followers of other religions, or humanists, would regard as defensible.

There is a special irony about this today, because the whole process is being reenacted with the same inextricable confusion of divine design and human aggression. While Israel claims its land as if by divine right, it comes up against the rights of other people who cannot be simply eliminated. The practical point is that an acceptance of covenant theology as valid in perpetuity does not mean that Israel's enemies can be justly stigmatized as God's enemies. For Israel (and those who would qualify as members of the new and expanded people of God, i.e., the Christian community) remains called to service, not to privilege.

For my present purpose it is sufficient to note that God revealed himself to Israel, at the dawn of its history and nationhood, only in so far as Israel was capable of receiving his revelation.[3] The carrying out of the

---

3. In Jesus Christ we see the best of Old Testament revelation confirmed and made perfect; but we shall see it as an oasis in the desert. This oasis metaphor sits in contrast to the traditional Christian community's dreary tale of a call to service that perversely has been interpreted as a guarantee of privilege. Indeed, the act of creation may have been in some sense effortless for God, but the Holy Spirit is still deeply involved in the struggle and is hard pressed.

covenant was expressed, from Israel's side, by law and by cult, especially by law; from God's side, it was expressed by righteousness and by loving-kindness or "covenant love" (*hesed*), understood as the love that inspired Yahweh to establish the covenant. The righteousness of Yahweh appears at first in his readiness to vindicate Israel against its enemies. The righteousness of Yahweh then assumes greater objectivity as the people of Israel realize that Yahweh will also chastise Israel for unrighteous behavior. Thus the people of Israel come to see Yahweh as the standard of righteousness by which human standards are to be measured.

The mercy or loving-kindness or "covenant love" of Yahweh is the key to the understanding of his character. This is kindness that goes beyond the minimum; it is faithful and steadfast. Yahweh has shown this love to Israel as his bride (Jer 2:2) and will show it again:

> I have loved you with an .everlasting love,
> so I am constant in my affection for you.
> (Jer 31:3)

> I will betroth you to myself forever,
> betroth you with integrity and justice,
> with tenderness and love;
> I will betroth you to myself with faithfulness
> and you will come to know Yahweh.
> (Hos 2:21–22)

It is clear that Jesus was born into a people who knew God, and knew him intimately. It would be patently false to say that Jesus revealed a God of love when the Jewish people had known only a God of power and dominion. (Indeed there is a sense in which Jesus reinforced the dominion of God by bringing in the kingdom; but he also brought the explicit teaching that God is Father of all.) Jesus revealed the Fatherhood of God in and through his life as the incarnate Son; and by his own loving obedience to the Father's will, and his costing service of the neighbor, he made it possible for humanity to see how the reign of God might be a reign of love, not a reign of terror.

New Testament theology sees God as the Father of our Lord Jesus Christ, just as developed Old Testament theology sees God as the Creator of the world and Lord of history, and Scholastic philosophy sees God as Being itself, *ipsum esse subsistens*. It is no over-simplification to say that Jesus revealed the Fatherhood of God, and in doing so revealed what human fatherhood might be. Childless himself, he was the perfect Son, revealing his Father's love in word and in deed.

So intense was the filial relationship of Jesus with his Father that it became the source of a new relationship of Christians to God as adopted sons. "The proof that you are sons is that God has sent the Spirit of his Son into our hearts: the Spirit that cries, 'Abba, Father'" (Gal 4:6).

This was true knowledge by experience. "They will know that I am Yahweh," said God in earlier times (e.g., Ps 46:10). "They will know that I am their Father," is the burden of the revelation through Jesus.

For St. Paul, God is "the Father of our Lord Jesus Christ, a gentle Father and the God of all consolation" (2 Cor 1:3; cf. 11:31, Rom 15:6). The Father in his loving-kindness has freely conceived the plan of humanity's salvation, the mystery kept hidden through all the ages (Eph 3:9). God has proved his love for us because "Christ died for us while we were still sinners" (Rom 5:8). St. Paul experienced the Father's love in experiencing redemption and liberation from sin and from bondage to the law through the grace of Jesus Christ.

The revelation of God as Father is oblique in Mark, but explicit in Matthew and Luke, especially in the Sermon on the Mount. We are to let our light shine before men, so that they may give the praise to our Father in heaven (Matt 5:16); prayer and almsgiving and fasting are to be done in secret, and our Father who sees all that is done in secret will reward us (6:4, 6, 18). We are not to worry about life, food, and clothing because our heavenly Father knows we need these things, and he even cares for the birds and the flowers (6:25–34). But we are to pray, in the sublime words of the "Our Father" (6:9–13); for our heavenly Father will forgive us if and only if we forgive others (6:14–15). We are to pray with confidence, for the Father's kindness exceeds that of any human father (7:11). But there is a warning: if we wish to enter the kingdom of heaven, we must do the Father's will (7:21).

The Father cares for every falling sparrow, and counts the hairs on our heads; but he can destroy body and soul in hell (10:28–31). We must call no one on earth our father because we have only one Father, and he is in heaven (23:9). One is reminded of Luke 2:49: "Did you not know that I must be busy with my Father's affairs?" and also of St. Francis of Assisi handing back his clothes to his father and acknowledging only his Father in heaven (see, too, Eph 3:14).

A moving passage, common to Mark (who has the word "Abba!"), Matthew, and Luke, is the prayer of Jesus in Gethsemane: "My Father, if it is possible, let this cup pass me by. Nevertheless, let it be as you, not I, would have it" (Matt 26:39; cf. Mark 14:36, Luke 22:42). This resolve is echoed at John 18:11, "Am I not to drink the cup that the Father has given me?" Thus all four Gospels imply that the Father's love is such that it can sustain Jesus through his scourging, crowning with thorns, and crucifixion.

In the discourse on the church, we are told not to despise the little ones, because their angels in heaven are continually in the presence of Jesus' Father in heaven (Matt 18:10). Also, it is never the will of our Father in heaven that one of these little ones should be lost (18:14). If two of us agree to ask anything at all, it will be granted by the Father (18:19); but, if we do not forgive our brother from our heart, the heavenly Father will hand us over to the torturers till we pay all our debt (18:23–35).

Both Matthew and Luke have the logion about the mutual knowledge of Father and Son already mentioned (Matt 11:25–27, Luke 10:21–24). Luke has his own fine references to the Fatherhood of God, notably in the parable of the two sons: "'your brother here was dead and has come to life; he was lost and is found'" (Luke 15:11–32); and the cry of Jesus as he breathed his last, "Father, into your hands I commit my spirit" (23:46; cf. Ps 31:5). The hands of the father are those of the breadwinner, strong and safe and rich in blessing; cf. Genesis 27:36, "Have you not kept a blessing for me too?"

If Matthew's Gospel proclaims the universal Fatherhood of God, the Gospel of John highlights the unique relationship of Jesus to God as his Father. More than a hundred times the author refers to the Father or has Jesus refer to the Father. In the prologue, the Word made flesh is called the only Son of the Father, full of grace and truth; and the only Son, nearest the Father's heart, the interpreter or translator of the Father (John 1:14, 18).

In the temple, Jesus lashes the money changers for turning his Father's house into a market (2:16). In the conversation with Nicodemus, we learn that "God loved the world so much that he gave his only Son, so that everyone who believes in him may not be lost but may have eternal life" (3:16).

The Samaritan woman is told that the hour is coming when true worshippers will worship the Father in spirit and truth (4:23); this is the pure ideal of religion that has captivated men's hearts but still eludes their grasp.

The Johannine Jesus justifies the Sabbath cure because his Father goes on working, and so does he; and it is here that the rich doctrine of Jesus' equal status and dignity with the Father begins to appear. Let us note, however, that this is no bolder than the Marcan claim that "the Son of Man is master even of the Sabbath" (Mark 2:28). But the conflict with his fellows (here "the Jews"!) is made sharper in John; they want to kill him because he not only breaks the Sabbath but makes himself God's equal. Jesus replies with one of the famous Johannine "discourses."

This particular discourse (John 5:18-47) is a totally self-authenticating claim to be sent by the Father and to have authority from the Father and power to be source of life and judge. There is an implicit appeal to the miracle, and an explicit appeal to the Scriptures; but, essentially, the passage presents a stark "Either/Or." This is what God's Son is 1ike; those who truly know God will recognize his Son whom he has sent. The others will not.

In the Eucharistic Discourse, it is the Father who gives the true bread from heaven, the bread that comes down from heaven and gives life to the world (6:32, 33) It is the Father who draws people to Jesus, and who gives eternal life to those who see the Son and believe in him (6:44, 40). The "Jews" think they know where he comes from; they know his father and mother. But Jesus insists that he has seen the Father, and he comes from God; and that no one else has seen the Father (6:41-46). Once again the Father is described as living, and as being the source of life:

> As I, who am sent by the living Father,
> myself draw life from the Father,
> so whoever eats me will draw life from me.
> (John 6:57)

For all their naive and primitive character, these polemical Johannine discourses contain beautiful insights about the mutual love of Father and Son. Not surprisingly, these insights are associated with the coming crucifixion: "I always do what pleases him" (7:29); "the Father loves me, because I lay down my life . . . this is the command I have been given by my Father" (10:17, 18).

There is much more said about the eternal Father in the Fourth Gospel, and I shall pursue the theme in my next chapter about the incarnate Son. What I have said here shows Jesus as the translator or interpreter introduced at John 1:18, and indicates why the Christian religion has conquered so many hearts. But I must enter a caveat against complacency.

The love of the Father is shown in action by Jesus, whom Peter rightly recognizes as the Holy One of God (John 6:69). Here perfect love has its perfect fulfillment. But the Johannine Jesus is a little too perfect. One almost feels that if Jesus had not cursed the fig tree (Mark 11:14) and massacred the Gadarene swine (Mark 5:13), someone would have had to invent these stories![4] By the same token, something has been lost of the Old Testament image of Yahweh, passionately fond of his faithless bride. The New Testament needs its basis in the Old, and was never meant to be without it. But if the Johannine Jesus is a little precocious, let us recall that the author of Hebrews tells us that Jesus "learnt to obey through suffering" and so was made perfect (Heb 5:8, 9). The Gospel of John, of course, is written from a post-resurrection perspective. With this warning, let us consider God revealed in Jesus Christ, the incarnate Son.

---

4. According to some modern scholars, it seems that someone did just that (i.e., invented these stories). See Meier, *Marginal Jew,* vol. 2, 884–96, 650–53; Lüdemann, *Great Deception,* 73–74.

13

God Revealed in Jesus Christ
The Incarnate Son

In the preceding chapter, I showed how in the Old Testament God was revealed to be the Father of Israel; and how in the New Testament Jesus perfected this revelation by showing that God is both Father of Jesus and Father of all men, "Go and find the brothers, and tell them: I am ascending to my Father and your Father, to my God and your God" (John 20:17). However, the background to the New Testament revelation of God the Son is also found in the Old Testament.[1]

Because we are considering the incarnation, it is necessary to concentrate on the idea of sonship as expressed in the Old Testament in connection with Israel and with the Davidic kingship.[2] I am not therefore directly concerned with the suggestion by Dr. Norman Pittenger that "it was a mistake to use the term Son . . . for the second hypostasis of the godhead as triune, for the Logos or Word."[3] But I note in passing that I have little sympathy with such intellectualism. Jesus was not a savant, but a worker, busy with his Father's affairs (Luke 2:49).

In the Psalms, God is described as "father of orphans, defender of widows" (68:5), and as a compassionate father of those who fear him:

---

1. This latter observation seems paradoxical because of the strict monotheism of the Jews. But Jewish monotheism should be seen in contrast with pagan polytheism, not in contrast with the deepest principles of Jewish religion.

2. If I were dealing with the Trinity, it would be necessary to look at the Old Testament teaching about the Word of God and the Wisdom of God, and to try to decide just what God was telling us about himself at this stage of revelation.

3. Pittenger, *Christology*, 13.

> As tenderly as a Father treats his children,
> so Yahweh treats those who fear him;
> he knows what we are made of,
> he remembers we are dust.
> (Ps 103:13, 14)

In the beautiful Psalm of Trito-Isaiah (Isa 63:7–64:11), God is seen as Father of his desolate people:

> For Abraham does not own us
> and Israel does not acknowledge us;
> you, Yahweh, yourself are our Father,
> Our Redeemer is your ancient name.
> (Isa 63:16)

God's fatherhood is founded on the act of creation (or, perhaps, formation) and not only on deliverance:

> And yet, Yahweh, you are our Father;
> we the clay, you the potter,
> we are all the work of your hand.
> (Isa 63:16)

The prophet Malachi sees God as the Father of all Jews, by creation: "Have we not all one Father? Did not one God create us?" (Mal 2: 10). He bases his teaching about mixed marriage and divorce on this fact.

The correlative of God's Fatherhood is the fact that men are God's children, his sons and daughters. Yet there are many stages by which this passes from being an abstract truth to an experienced reality. The correlative of Creator is creature, and it is not at all clear that a creature can be a son or a daughter of its Creator. The position of Christian theology is that there is in fact one natural Son of God, namely Jesus, and that men and women are called to be brothers and sisters of Jesus, sons and daughters of God by adoption.

This divine Sonship, which in Jesus is translated into human form, has been expressed by anticipation in the sonship of Israel. God took action to make Israel his son long before the Jews would seem to have had a clear idea of creation out of nothing, long before they knew themselves to be Yahweh's creatures in the strict sense of the word.[4] This fact immediately faces us with an existential problem: Can a creature ever be a son?

---

4. Creation *ex nihilo* is first mentioned in the Bible at 2 Maccabees 7:28. McEleney, "1–2 Maccabees."

For Jesus, let us remember, is not a creature! The point must be deferred to my next chapter; I simply note here that it is the Spirit who assures us of sonship: "The Spirit himself and our spirit bear united witness that we are children of God. And if we are children we are heirs as well: heirs of God and coheirs with Christ, sharing his sufferings so as to share his glory" (Rom 8:16, 17). For a creature, the way to sonship is through suffering.

The covenant between Yahweh and Israel implied that he adopted them as his people. "I will adopt you as my own people, and I will be your God" (Exod 6:7). Because of the corporate personality of Israel, the nation of Israel could also be adopted by Yahweh as his son. "Israel is my first-born son. I ordered you to let my son go to offer me worship. You refuse to let him go. So be it! I shall put your first-born to death" (Exod 4:22, 23).

In the eighty-second Psalm those who dispense justice are called gods, and also princes. God dispenses justice to them in turn, and says:

> I once said, "You too are gods,
> sons of the Most High, all of you."
> (Ps 82:6)

The passage is used at John 10:34 in Jesus' polemic with "the Jews." But it seems to incorporate Canaanite myth into the Yahwist religion.[5]

Hosea, prophet of Yahweh's conjugal love for Israel and of his unshakable fidelity, foresees a great future in which the sons of Israel, numerous as the sand on the seashore, in the very place where they were told, "You are no people of mine," will be called, "The sons of the living God" (Hos 2:1). This sonship is founded on God's unfailing love for Israel:

> When Israel was a child I loved him,
> and I called my son out of Egypt.
> (Hos 11:1)

In spite of Israel's infidelity and the inevitable punishment which follows, God cannot abandon his love:

> Ephraim, how could I part with you?
> Israel, how could I give you up? . . .
> My heart recoils from it,
> my whole being trembles at the thought.
> I will not give rein to my fierce anger,

---

5. Murphy, "Psalms."

> I will not destroy Ephraim again,
> for I am God, not man:
> I am the Holy One in your midst
> and have no wish to destroy.
> (Hos 11:8, 9)

The prophet goes on to describe the return from exile, when Yahweh will lead Israel home again, roaring like a lion: "How he will roar!" (Hos 11:10).

In monarchical times, the king became the representative and embodiment of Israel's corporate personality. Hence he too was adopted by Yahweh as a son. This is particularly true of David, who received the promise of perpetual rule: "Your House and your sovereignty will always stand secure before me and your throne be established forever" (2 Sam 7:16). Because of the divine promise made to David for his dynasty, the holy person of the king as Yahweh's "Anointed," installed on his holy mountain, had the dignity of adoptive sonship:

> Let me proclaim Yahweh's decree;
> he has told me, "You are my son,
> today I have become your father.
> Ask and I will give you the nations for your heritage,
> the ends of the earth for your domain."
> (Ps 2:7, 8)

The oracle uttered to David by the prophet Nathan was the foundation of royal messianism. In Psalm 110, the king is credited with a mysterious birth, and with everlasting priesthood:

> Royal dignity was yours from the day you were born,
> on the holy mountains,
> royal from the womb, from the dawn of your earliest days.
> Yahweh has sworn an oath which he never will retract,
> "You are a priest of the order of Melchizedek, and forever."
> (Ps 110:3, 4)

The seventy-second Psalm shows the nature of royal messianism, the hopes that were held out for the king, at once political and yet strangely open to the future. It is hoped that the king will rule justly, at peace, defending the poor; that he will enjoy life forever, and worldwide rule. It is Yahweh, the God of Israel, who entertains these plans for David's line. Because the lives of the poor and the feeble will be precious in the king's eyes, his people will bless him and pray for him. The courtly style is adapted to proclaim God's final plan for his people.

Both at his baptism and at his transfiguration Jesus is proclaimed the beloved Son, according to Mark. At his baptism in the Jordan by John, Jesus sees the heavens open and the Spirit descend on him: "And a voice came from heaven, 'You are my Son, the Beloved; my favor rests on you'" (Mark 1:11).[6]

At the transfiguration, there is a voice from the cloud, "'This is my Son, the Beloved. Listen to him'" (Mark 9:7). Both these passages echo the first song of the servant of Yahweh:

> Here is my servant whom I uphold,
> my chosen one in whom my soul delights.
> (Isa 42:1)

The theme of the beloved son can be traced back to the story of Abraham and Isaac (Gen 22:2). It has redemptive meaning, "God did not spare his own Son, but gave him up to benefit us all" (Rom 8:32). The Father takes delight in his Son and Servant, because the Son is ready to give his life for his sheep (John 8:29, 10:17). The true son is the one who does his father's will (Matt 21:28–31).

That Jesus is the eternal Son of God through whom the world was made is taught most clearly in Hebrews and in the Gospel of John. For the author of Hebrews, Jesus is the Son whom God "has appointed to inherit everything and through whom he made everything there is" (Heb 1:2). A Scholastic would understandably hasten to add: "except himself!" The Greek text has *tous aionas*, "the worlds." The author of Hebrews goes on to demonstrate, by the "encyclopedic" method of exegesis (piling text upon text with very little comment) that the Son is greater than the angels. This is the full articulation of the message implicit in Mark 13:32: "But as for that day or hour, nobody knows it, neither the angels of heaven, nor the Son; no one but the Father."

The burden of Hebrews, chapter one, is that the Son is "as far above the angels as the title which he has inherited is higher than their own name" (Heb 1:4). But he who has inherited these titles is "the radiant light of God's glory and the perfect copy of his nature, sustaining the universe by his powerful command" (1:3). These attributes require a metaphysical explanation, for they belong to Wisdom itself (Wis 7:26). To clinch the

---

6. On "Spirit" Christology, see del Colle's *Christ and the Spirit* and Kasper's, *Jesus*, 251.

matter, the words of Psalm 102:25–27 are applied to the Son: "It is you, Lord, who laid earth's foundations in the beginning, the heavens are the work of your hands . . . But yourself, you never change and your years are unending."

The rest of Hebrews develops the theme of Christ as priest, mediator, the pioneer and perfecter of our faith; Christ suffering and exalted, "faithful as a son, and as the master in the house," not as a servant, like Moses (Heb 3:2–6). As Son of God, Jesus is the supreme high priest who has gone through to the highest heaven (Heb 4:14). Although he was Son, he learned obedience through the things he suffered (5:8; Dr. Norman Pittenger happily suggests "underwent" or "experienced" as a better translation of *epathen* here).[7]

It is clear by now that the themes of obedience and love come together in the expression of Sonship in Jesus. To "obey" means, in practice, to do what you are told to do, to carry out someone else's bidding. In terms of internal assent, it means to will what someone else wills, to accept the norm and principle of one's willing from another. For an intelligent human being, a blind or mechanical obedience is a castration. Obedience inspired by love is another matter. That the obedience of Jesus was inspired by love is evident from his words, "I always do what pleases him" (John 8:29), and "My food is to do the will of the one who sent me, and to complete his work" (John 4:34). This suggests a real hunger to obey (cf. Matt 4:4; Luke 4:4), and the words should be measured against the task, as they were in Gethsemane (Mark 14:36 and parallels).

The motives of love and obedience are brought together in John as a prelude to the story of the Passion: The world must be brought to know that I love the Father and that I am doing exactly what the Father told me (John 14:31).

Indeed, the entire life of Jesus can be seen as an act of obedience. The author of Hebrews saw it thus, putting on to the lips of Jesus the words of the Septuagint version of Psalm 40:8: "I said, . . . 'God, here I am! I am coming to obey your will'" (Heb 10:7).

The theme is present in Luke 4:18–19, where Jesus reads from Isaiah: "He has sent me to bring the good news to the poor, to proclaim liberty to captives and to the blind new sight, to set the downtrodden free . . ." (cf. Isa 61:1, 2).

---

7. Pittenger, *Christology*, 37.

The work or task that Jesus has received from the Father is a dominant theme in the Fourth Gospel. The "works" or miracles of Jesus are part of this task: "The works my Father has given me to carry out, these same works of mine testify that the Father has sent me" (John 5:36).

There is an urgency about Jesus' need to work: "As long as the day lasts I must carry out the work of the one who sent me" (John 9:4). This sentiment is reminiscent of Mark 1:38, "Let us go elsewhere . . . so that I can preach there too, because that is why I came." Finally, the Johannine Christ can say, even before the crucifixion: "I have glorified you on earth and finished the work that you gave me to do" (John 17:4).

Jesus underlines the point by saying on the cross, "It is accomplished" (John 19:20).

Obedience can appear to be a purely human virtue that is in no way relevant to divine Sonship. However, the Fourth Gospel brings out the subtlety of the Son's obedience to the Father: "The Son can do nothing by himself; he can do only what he sees the Father doing: and whatever the Father does the Son does too" (John 5:19).

But Father and Son are joined together by love: "For the Father loves the Son and shows him everything he does himself" (John 5:20a).

This showing is translated on to the human level: "And he will show him even greater things than these, works that will astonish you" (John 5:20b).

The relationship implied here can only be expressed in the paradoxical sentences, "The Father is greater than I" (John 14:28) and "The Father and I are one" (*hen*, i.e., one thing) (John 10:30).

The complete "compenetration" of Father and Son is implied by the oft repeated sentence, "The Father is in me and I am in the Father" (John 10:38; 14:10, 11; cf. 6:57, "I, who am sent by the living Father, myself draw life from the Father"). Such divine compenetration is translated on to the human level by complete and utter trust: "Father, I thank you for hearing my prayer. I knew indeed that you always hear me, but I speak for the sake of those who stand round me, so that they may believe it was you who sent me" (John 11:42).

This trust is available to us too: "Anything you ask for from the Father he will grant in my name" (John 16:23; cf. Matt 18:19).

I have already referred to the uniqueness of Jesus as the true Servant, contrasting favorably with the people of God both before and after him. But it is necessary to look at this more closely. For here is found the trans-

God Revealed in Jesus Christ

lation of unique divine Sonship, even though it carries with it the risk of irrelevance, a risk that is sadly underlined by the fate of the Son of Man who, per Bonhoeffer's fine phrase, was edged out of the world and on to the cross.

As vagrant Son of Man, with nowhere to lay his head (Matt 8:20), Jesus is sublimely indifferent to the middle class virtues of thrift, circumspection, and a careful regard for property. He teaches people to use their talents (Matt 25:14–30) and to let their light shine before men (Matt 5:15, 16). But he urges them not to lay up treasure on earth (Matt 6:19) and to give to those who ask (Matt 5:42; Luke 6:29, 30); he points to the birds of the air and the lilies of the field in order to teach people not to fret over food and clothing (Matt 6:25–34; Luke 12:22–31); he says it is impossible to serve God and money (Matt 6:24; Luke 16:13).

Inevitably, the apostles, in building up the Christian community, stress the duty of work. "We gave you a rule when we were with you: not to let anyone have food if he refuses to do any work" (2 Thess 3:10). Paul bases this precept on his own example and that of his fellow workers: "We worked night and day, slaving and straining, so as not to be a burden on any of you" (3:8). But it seems a short step from this admirable zeal to modern capitalist society and the domain of White Anglo-Saxon Protestantism. Jesus cannot be claimed as the champion of nonworking hippies, since he clearly pulled his weight. But there are depths to his teaching that escape human classification. That is why he can say, "Come to me all you who labor and are overburdened, and I will give you rest" (Matt 11:28).

Again, on the subject of violence, Jesus seems strangely unaware of the need to repay violence with violence, a blow on the cheek with a blow on the cheek (Matt 5:39; Luke 6:29; cf. John 18:22, 23; Acts 23:2, 3), a hydrogen bomb with a hydrogen bomb, and so on. When a Samaritan village refused to receive him, he was not impressed by the suggestion of James and John that they should call down fire from heaven to burn the people up, after the manner of Elijah (Luke 9:54, 56; cf. 2 Kings 1:1–18). According to a logion that was present in some of the ancient manuscripts, and which was retained by the Authorized Version and by Ronald Knox, but not by more recent versions, Jesus would have replied, "You do not understand what spirit it is you share. The Son of Man has come to save men's lives, not to destroy them" (Luke 9:55, 56, Ronald Knox New Testament). I mention this here because of the interesting contrast it provides with Peter's words to Sapphira: "So you and your husband have agreed to put the Spirit of the Lord to the test! . . . You hear those footsteps? They have just been to bury your husband; they will carry you out, too" (Acts 5:9); whereupon the wretched woman fell dead.

Once again, Peter is trying to organize a church. But it seems clear that the Holy Spirit acts differently in the presence of Jesus and in his absence. Indeed, we remain confronted by a revelation that exceeds all human wisdom and defies all codification into a set of rules. No doubt moral theologians will go on making rules about the use of the hydrogen bomb. But it is Jesus, and not the moral theologians, who will save us from the hydrogen bomb. Jesus does so not by a miraculous intervention but by his work within the hearts of men. Let us, once again, remember that it is the mission and vocation of the Son of Man to be edged out of the world and on to the cross.

A third theme on which we can see the transcendence of Jesus is forgiveness. Here I wish to transcend the Catholic-Protestant controversy about justification. Let us instead understand Jesus as God in the flesh, and recall the fact that only God is big enough to forgive sin.

What emerges unmistakably from the conduct of Jesus toward sinners is that forgiveness is a service, a boon, and a benefit, rather than an imposition. Seeing the faith of those who brought the paralytic to him, Jesus said to the afflicted man, "My child, your sins are forgiven" (Mark 2:5). Jesus went on to complete the cure. The evangelist is intent on the apologetic value of this event, and perhaps Jesus was too, for we have no reason to suppose that the author is mistaken or lying. But the incident needs to be seen in the whole context of Jesus' ministry of healing and exorcism. Unquestionably, the Son of Man has come to minister, not to be ministered to; and forgiveness, genuine forgiveness, which really puts man right with God, is part of this service.

The conduct of Jesus cannot be fitted into the framework of a formal doctrine of forgiveness, a doctrine that is at least as popular with Protestants as with Catholics. With regard to the adulterous woman, Jesus failed to elicit from her either an expression of sorrow or a firm purpose of amendment (or even a commitment to faith). He simply refused to condemn her, detached himself from the whole business but without ceasing to care, and told her to go away and not to sin any more (John 8:1–11). At the same time, his attitude to the accusers (verse 7) shows that he was far from being insensitive to the moral values involved.

Here again, one must pay tribute to the church for two thousand years of fighting against sin. If the church has sometimes seemed to be retaining more sins than it was forgiving (John 20:23), and even multiplying sins by multiplying laws (Rom 4:15), that is because the church is not God. Let us remember that, as Jesus has shown, only God is big enough to forgive sin. It is ironic that Jesus should reserve his fiercest indignation for that very hypocrisy that must accompany any legal system legalistically interpreted (Matt 23:1–39; Luke 20:45–47, 11:37–54). But it remains true that the Catholic Church offers to millions of people the only objective basis they have for feeling that they are not destined for eternal damnation. That fact must, like charity, cover a multitude of sins.

The uniqueness of Jesus is summed up in one word: Servant. Jesus is the true Servant, the Servant of Yahweh and the Man for others. He gave his disciples an authority of service (Luke 22: 24–27), and showed them how to exercise it (John 13:1–17). As a result, we are tasked with service.

The truth of the matter is that we all pay lip service to the idea of service, though very few of us have any taste for real service. Suffice it to say that the vast majority of us prefer the fictitious variety of service: "I am your servant, and God help you if you don't let me serve you in the way that I want to."

Against this attitude, the cross is raised with its stark message of defeat in victory and victory in defeat. No one could have guessed that this is how God would appear in the flesh: scourged, mocked, crucified; in a word, defeated. Yet we feel in our bones that it is right; and, as we survey the human world, inside and outside our own hearts, with its inane pomposities and idle fictions, we know that nothing else could be right.

This completes my analysis of "God revealed in Jesus Christ: the incarnate Son." I have tried to show the unique status of Jesus as presenting God to us and transcending the Jewish people before him and the church after him. It remains now to consider the fulfillment of human redemption through the work of the Holy Spirit.

14

God Revealed Through Jesus Christ
The Holy Spirit

For the third and last time, allow me to insist that I am not writing about the Trinity but about the incarnation. Let us then concern ourselves with the work of the Holy Spirit in relation to the incarnation that is understood as the translation of God's Word or uttered Truth into human form. Likewise, I am not writing about the church, and so I shall not consider the role of the Holy Spirit as quite literally the life and soul of the Christian Church. Even so, I cannot avoid touching on church doctrine, and I will do so as succinctly as possible when it is required.

The translation of the Truth into human form had as its purpose the communication of meaning, understanding, life. But such communication has to be internally imparted or elicited within each individual. Because it is not possible to take ideas from one's own mind and place them directly into the minds of others, we must resort to "education." How many educators (and theologians!) have come to grief over this fact! Now the whole of God's revelation of himself up to the incarnation can be seen as a preparation for Jesus, the imparting of certain hints which would enable men to accept Jesus. In this regard, education means a drawing forth of what is potentially already present. By the same token, the whole work of Jesus can be seen as giving us the essential hints that we needed in order to work things out for ourselves.

This is a bold statement, likely to sever all communication between author and reader. So let me say at once that this statement is based on the teachings in the New Testament; a statement that is my interpretation of the words of the Johannine Christ:

God Revealed Through Jesus Christ

> It is for your own good that I am going
> *because unless I go,*
> *the Advocate will not come to you;*
> but if I do go,
> I will send him to you.
> (John 16:7; my emphasis)

The most astonishing thing about the Christian religion is that Jesus, having become man and having conquered death, almost immediately left the scene. One has to ask: In the name of God, why? Superstitious answers abound, though they can be reduced to a simple refrain: It was to make faith more difficult! Based on what I have already said, it should be clear that I brush such ideas aside with contempt.

In truth, the answer to this question has been given in John: Jesus had to go in order to send the Advocate, the Spirit of truth (John 14:17, 15:26, 16:13) to us. Once we leave aside the beautiful but mythological language in which this fact is stated, we see the absolute necessity of this truth. One often hears the joking remark: What would Jesus say if he returned to earth today? What interest, if any, would he take in the Pope and the Archbishop of Canterbury? Whose "side" would he be on? And so on. These lighthearted questions veil an important truth. The idea that Jesus might have stayed on as a kind of religious consultant, to sort out our theological and moral problems, is not consistent with what we know of the life of Jesus himself. Simply stated, human problems simply do not get solved in simple ways. Human beings both learn and teach as a result of struggle; it is a development process that enables individuals to attain maturity. Jesus, having been made perfect, had literally nothing more that he could teach us through the sort of human personal contact that he had with men in the days of his flesh (John 20:17, "Do not cling to me"). The rest was up to the Holy Spirit: it was for the Spirit to bring to our minds all we needed to know in order to understand and complete the work of Jesus himself. Once again, I offer this opinion with great confidence because it seems to me that any other explanation of the departure of Jesus either falls short of the full Christian faith, because it questions or minimizes the physical reality of his resurrection, or verges on the magical and so threatens to reduce religious belief to mere superstition.

So Jesus leaves us in order to send us the Advocate, or Spirit, of truth. What then is the task of this Advocate? A fairly straightforward one, it seems: "But when the Spirit of truth comes he will lead you to the complete truth, ... and he will tell you of the things to come" (John 16:13).

This translation "complete truth" is better than "all truth" (Authorized Version, Ronald Knox New Testament), because "complete truth" implies the compact unity of truth, based on the simplicity of God who is subsistent Truth. In any case, one thinks here of a sort of "basic" or "essential" truth (whatever that may be, for the Holy Spirit is still at work!), rather than of particular truths, which would seem to be indefinite in number.

It is essential to realize that the Holy Spirit's teaching is anchored in Jesus' own revelation to us:

> The Advocate, the Holy Spirit,
> whom the Father will send in my name,
> will teach you everything
> and remind you of all I have said to you.
> (John 14:26)

Hence we have soul-searching discussions about the development of doctrine, about Scripture (and tradition) as one source or two sources of revelation, about the sense in which the deposit of faith was closed with the death of the last apostle, and so on.

Perhaps it is inevitable that, as a Roman Catholic "innovator" (always supposing that there is anything new under the sun; cf. Eccl 1:9), I should have given a certain amount of thought to these questions. But such questions remain among the thorniest problems in the whole of theology. If there is any sign of a consensus among theologians, it would seem to favor organic development, which must be related to Scripture as the objectively verifiable and permanent Word of God, and which can never, of course, amount to a replacement of the revelation given in and through Jesus Christ by a new revelation.

Such questions bring me back to the underpinnings of translation Christology. I believe that translation Christology satisfies all the criteria listed in my previous paragraph. In particular, I find it gratifying that translation Christology is related to the ongoing life of the church in the Holy Spirit, and especially to the sound devotion to the heart of Jesus expressed by the fathers of the church, by Protestants and by Catholics, and emphasized, with some baroque flourishes, in the writings of St. Margaret Mary Alacoque. Yet translation Christology is anchored in the Scriptures, from John 1:18, 1 John 1:1–4, and Colossians 1:15 onward.

God Revealed Through Jesus Christ

Because translation Christology is simply an attempt to interpret Jesus and his revelation, we must then consider the work of the Holy Spirit. The work of the Holy Spirit, in completing the translation of God's Truth into human form, expounds it, explains it and makes it live in the hearts and lives of the faithful. I want to emphasize that such work cannot merely involve conceptual knowledge or understanding. It involves experiential knowledge, biblical "knowledge" that includes love, what St. Paul meant when he said that he wanted to know nothing but Jesus, and then only as the crucified Christ (1 Cor 2:2). It is in this light that Paul says, "For me to live is Christ" (Phil 1:21, Authorized Version) and "I live; yet not I, but Christ liveth in me" (Gal 2:20, Authorized Version).

Because Christ is to live in us, we are to be children of God. The supreme achievement of the Holy Spirit, then, is making us children of our heavenly Father. "The proof that you are sons is that God has sent the Spirit of his Son into our hearts: the Spirit that cries 'Abba, Father,' and it is this that makes you a son, you are not a slave anymore; and if God has made you son, then he has made you heir" (Gal 4:6-7). We remain children of God by living the life of the spirit (Rom 8:1-13). This means being conformed to the image of Christ. For Paul, this means living according to the spirit (the divine element) and not according to the flesh (the human element). For John, it means, above all, loving one another:

> We have passed out of death and into life,
> and of this we can be sure
> because we love our brothers.
> (1 John 3:14)

In completing the work of Jesus, the Holy Spirit also reveals himself to us. As the Johannine Jesus promised, the Father and he come to dwell in us (John 14:23) and communicate their Spirit to us. It is as well that I linger on this fact, for here the work of Jesus is finally completed; for here we live together in the Spirit, and already God begins to be all in all (1 Cor 15:28).

By a happy coincidence, the Roman Catholic liturgical year is largely reckoned from the feast of Pentecost. I say coincidence because there can be little doubt that this was done to honor the church itself and not expressly to honor the Holy Spirit. Recall that the church used to reckon its birthday from Whitsunday or Pentecost.

The Holy Spirit is often called the "neglected Person" of the Trinity. He is neglected because he has never attained human form, either through anthropomorphism or through incarnation. The neglect was already present in the apostolic church; the disciples whom Paul met at Ephesus "were never even told there was such a thing as a Holy Spirit" (Acts 19:2). But there was an explanation: they had received the baptism of John, not the baptism of Jesus.

It is true that the Holy Spirit reveals himself by concealing himself; that is, his presence is revealed by our ability to say "Abba!" or "Our Father" to the Father of Jesus, and by our ability to confess that Jesus is the Christ. Yet the church has devoted one of its most beautiful hymns, the "Veni, Sancte Spiritus," to the Holy Spirit, as the Sequence for Pentecost Sunday in the Roman Missal.[1] In this Sequence, the Holy Spirit is called Father of the poor, Bestower of gifts, Light of hearts; he is greeted as our rest from toil, our solace amid grief, our refreshment in the noonday heat. He is asked to wash away all that is sordid, to water the clay that is barren, to heal what is diseased; to bend our rigid will, to warm our cold heart, to govern our devious steps. Finally, he is asked to bestow on his faithful, trusting people the sevenfold gift of grace, so that they may come to everlasting joy.

There have been signs of a renewed awareness of the Holy Spirit in the Roman Catholic Church, and indeed in all the churches in the years since Pope John XXIII called the Second Vatican Council and so initiated his *aggiornamento*[2]. This ferment augurs well for the immediate future of Christianity; for, where the Holy Spirit is active and known to be active, great things can happen. It is probable, almost certain, that theology will have only a small part to play in the developments that lie immediately ahead. In recent times, the emphasis has been on the medium and not the message, the style and not the content, the music and not the words. I would not accept the view that the words do not matter anymore, that only the music counts. But I would go so far as to state that if you get the music right the words will come right in the end: "The man whose life is true comes to the light, so that his deeds may be seen for what they are, deeds done in God" (John 3:21, Ronald Knox New Testament).

1. *Missale Romanum*, 367.

2. This sentence reflects the date of my PhD thesis in 1971, within a decade of the Second Vatican Council, which took place in the early 1960s.

I, too, have neglected the Holy Spirit in favor of the Father and the Son. But then my intent was to write about the incarnation. I turn now to the incarnation realized in fact, and the incarnation fulfilled in history.

15

The Incarnation Realized in Fact
Christogenesis

The Word-consciousness of Jesus was subject to development: The incarnation took time.

It would seem that this view can claim the authority of St. Peter and St. Paul. St. Paul began the Epistle to the Romans: "From Paul, a servant of Christ Jesus who has been called to be an apostle, and specially chosen to preach the Good News that God promised long ago through his prophets in the scriptures.

"This news is about the Son of God who, according to the human nature he took, was a descendant of David: it is about Jesus Christ our Lord who, in the order of the spirit, the spirit of holiness that was in him, was proclaimed [*oristhentos*, designated] Son of God in all his power [*en dunamei*] through his resurrection from the dead [*ex anastaseos nekron*]" (Rom 1:1–4).

The construction of this passage is very involved in the Greek text. The passage hardly favors a "two stage" Christology of pure Adoptionism; rather it seems to require that incarnation itself develops over time.[1] According to Acts, St. Peter on the day of Pentecost concluded his speech with the words: "For this reason the whole House of Israel can be certain that God has made [*epoiesen*] this Jesus whom you crucified both Lord and Christ" (Acts 2:36). Once again the implication for theology is that the incarnation attained its fulfillment after the crucifixion.

---

1. For a deeper discussion of the problems raised by this passage, see Fitzmyer, "Letter," 15–16. Note also that the New English Bible translates *en dunamei* as "by a mighty act."

I think it is a mistake to try to read back a theology of Adoptionism into these passages. The Adoptionists distinguished in Christ two Sons: a natural Son of God who was the eternal Word and an adopted son of God who was the man Jesus Christ. This view was rejected by the early church as heretical. In Christ there was but one Son, the eternal Son of God, only begotten of the Father according to his divine nature, and firstborn of all creation according to his human nature. Neither St. Peter nor St. Paul taught otherwise. This was and remains the teaching of the church. The Adoptionists, however, recognized that the incarnation took time, and in this they were at one with the teaching of St. Peter and St. Paul.

A modern Roman Catholic testimony to this fact comes from Schillebeeckx: "But this incarnation of God the Son is a reality which grows. It is not complete in a matter of a moment; for example, at Jesus' conception in Mary's womb or at his birth. The Incarnation is not merely a Christmas event. To be man is a process of becoming man; Jesus' manhood grew throughout his earthly life, finding its completion in the supreme moment of the Incarnation, his death, resurrection and exaltation."[2]

It should be noted that even as a child Jesus was conscious of his unique Sonship. At the age of twelve he said to his parents: "Did you not know that I must be busy with my Father's affairs?" (Luke 2:49).[3] He was from the first predestined to be the Word incarnate and no other person. But the elevation of his human consciousness into that of the Word, which began in his tender years, was subject to development and intensification, as I shall presently indicate.

Of course my theory requires no mechanical intervention of God to produce the incarnation. The seeds from which all things, including the God-man, were to emerge were already sown in the chaos. From the very beginning, creation was pregnant with rational consciousness, pregnant with Christ. As man emerged from nonhuman antecedents, so Christ emerged from the expectation of his people.[4] Indeed, he emerged as the One desired by all nations, in answer to man's aspirations to share the life of God. At the same time, under the providence of God, Christ emerged

---

2. Schillebeeckx, *Christ the Sacrament*, 20.

3. I would not claim that the boy Jesus had formal theological knowledge of his divine Sonship (Brown, *Birth*, 471–96). But it is unlikely that Jesus was not told about the manner of his conception.

4. Note the messianic significance of Ecclesiasticus 24:16: "I [Wisdom] *have taken root* in a privileged people, in the Lord's property, in his inheritance" (my emphasis).

as the masterpiece of the all-wise Creator. It is God who first loves man, and who gives man the means of loving in return. But God needed no mechanical intervention or contrivance in order to reveal himself to men.

The insight of Jesus into the Trinity was so sure in its aim, the truth he lived so clear in its enunciation (though much is owed for its full development to Christian thinkers from St. Paul and St. John onward), that we speak of vision and not mere faith in this connection.[5] Jesus spoke and acted with authority, as one who sees, not as one who gropes in the dark (John 3:11). Yet this clarity of vision emerged from the darkness under the providence of God: the light shone in darkness and the darkness was not able to master it (John 1:5). Such was the intricacy and the grandeur of the divine plan for man's salvation.

If we possessed an exact chronological record of Christ's words and deeds, we might be able to follow in detail his growth into the fullness of Word-consciousness. As it is, we can but piece together the scattered fragments that we have, and sketch the outline of a Christogenesis.[6] This, I shall do. But in so doing, I shall not indulge in "biologism" or "psychologism"; rather I shall simply give flesh and blood to the statement, "Jesus grew to manhood, indeed to God-manhood." Note that Jesus is eternally God, but that he grew to God-manhood. In so far as I follow any chronological order at all, it is that of *The Gospel Story* by Ronald Knox and Ronald Cox, which was in turn based on the work of M.-J. Lagrange, OP.[7]

The virgin birth of Jesus was, I think, a key factor in both his Messiah-consciousness and his Son-consciousness.[8] The reference in Isaiah 7:14 to

---

5. But see Cullmann's *Christology* on the "faith" of Jesus according to Hebrews 12:2 (Jesus is the "pioneer and perfecter of our faith") and also on the development of Jesus' interior life according to Hebrews 5:8 (Jesus "learned obedience") and Hebrews 2:10 (Jesus was "made perfect" through suffering).

6. I owe the word "Christogenesis" to the epoch-making work of Teilhard de Chardin, *Phenomenon of Man*.

7. Knox and Cox, *Gospel Story*. But note that the Gospels do not give a chronological account of the life of Jesus, nor do they discuss his psychological states in any direct manner. As Meier says, "Without a sense of 'before and after,' any biography in the modern sense—and indeed any sketch of the psychological or religious development of Jesus—is impossible." *Marginal Jew*, vol. 1, 42. No doubt a rigorous scholar like Meier would regard this chapter of mine as partly "novel writing." So be it!

8. More accurately, virginal conception. I accept that as far as history takes us Jesus was probably born in Nazareth and Joseph was his biological father: Bond, *Historical Jesus*, 67–72. But I here cling to the faith of my childhood until such time as it may be proved to be impossible.

The Incarnation Realized in Fact

this phenomenon is obscure and ambiguous; only the Septuagint Greek text contains explicitly the word "virgin" (*parthenos*), which is quoted at Matthew 2:23. It may not be merely fanciful to see here a convergence of cultures, an influence of the Greek theory of the hermaphrodite on Jewish thought, which had no special cult of virginity. Galilee was semipagan anyway. But once again, the determining factor is genetic. The genealogy of Jesus was prepared by God with the infinite skill of all-creating intelligence. Given a unique moral and physical disposition, Mary's desire to be the mother of the Messiah, which she shared with every pious girl of her nation, may have been instrumental in God's design in producing the phenomenon of parthenogenesis.

It is interesting that science is now, for the first time, able to consider parthenogenesis in humans as being a serious possibility.[9] The Christian interest in considering this possibility is not a rationalist one; rather this interest is the need to safeguard the integrity of the incarnation. Thus, it has been suggested by Cletus Wessels, OP, (as a tenable opinion) that God may have created the centrioles and chromosomes necessary to make the conception of a male parthenogenone possible.[10] But this view seems inadequate. For then the human nature of Jesus would have been partly from our race and partly a special creation; this makes Christ a hybrid, and endangers his work of redemption.[11] So a true incarnation seems to require that the centrioles and chromosomes came from Mary's body. This opinion would entail the consequence that Jesus may have resembled his Mother as few other sons have done in history; a point of view that accords both with Catholic piety and with early Christian iconography.[12]

---

9. Beatty, *Parthenogenesis*; Spurway, "Virgin Births," in *Lancet*, 967–68 and also in *New Statesman and Nation*, 651.

10. Wessels, *Mother of God*, 155–56; on theories of sex determination, see Beatty, *Parthenogenesis*, 103. For a conservative evangelical view of the virgin birth, see Laubach, *Did Mary Tell Jesus Her Secret?*

11. The late Professor E. L. Mascall suggested to me that this view would logically involve some form of the Apollinarian heresy, Christ's humanity being partly supplied by the Word. But he seems to have changed his mind, judging from the reference to his *Theology* in Goulder "Paradox and Mystification," 54–56.

12. In addition to the problem mentioned here, the Rev. Malory Makower, in a private communication dated January 19, 1970, drew my attention to the danger of abnormality of a parthenogenone through the presence of unmasked deleterious recessive genes. I think that the physical concomitants of the immaculate conception of Mary herself could well include freedom from deleterious recessive genes; but I must leave further discussion of this point to expert geneticists. I would just add that, both at his conception and

The psychological factors involved in the virginal conception of Jesus are so important here that I feel I must quote a rather long passage from St. Aelred (twelfth century). As St. Aelred shows, piety and psychology are not necessarily implacable enemies:

> Perhaps at that very time when the angel came to her she held Isaias in her hands. Perhaps she was then meditating on that prophecy: "Behold, a Virgin shall conceive, and bear a Son, and His name shall be called Emmanuel" (Isa 7:14). Methinks that in that very hour that prophecy had caused a most lovely contest in her heart. I fancy that when she read that a virgin should one day give birth to the Son of God, a secret and timid wish rose in her heart that she might be that favored one; and then again she thought that she was altogether unworthy of so great a boon. So charity struggled with fear, and devotion with humility. Now she almost despaired in her great fear, and then, out of the abundance of her great desire, she could not but hope. Devotion urged her to aspire; but at once her great humility bade her check her aspirations. And in the midst of this hesitation, this fluctuation, this desire, the angel enters in and says: "Hail, full of grace."[13]

The Virgin Birth meant two things in the human consciousness of Jesus. First, it provided the certainty that Jesus was the Messiah. The prophecy of Isaiah could be clearly interpreted after the event: there was no room for doubt or speculation about this aspect of his destiny. Second, and far more fundamental, the lack of a human father gave the physical and psychological basis of Jesus' unique vision of the Father as first his own Father; and second the Father of all mankind. This lack of a human father provided the basis of his Son-consciousness. This assertion is strengthened by the fact that the Aramaic word *Abba*, with which Jesus referred to his Father, expresses an intimate familiarity such as a human child might feel toward his human father.

So I vindicate St. Luke's Christology against all the theologians, conservative, progressive, and radical: "'The Holy Spirit will come upon you' the angel answered 'and the power of the Most High will cover you with

---

at his resurrection, the biological constitution of Jesus appears to escape the limits of our present knowledge. Perhaps it will take a hundred or a thousand more years before geneticists can begin to understand God's work in the incarnation of his Son. The science of genetics is in its infancy. But it is poised to unlock the secrets of the universe.

13. *Mount Carmel,* Vol. 2, 115. I simply do not know whether Mary would have known the Greek (Septuagint) text of Isaiah 7:14.

its shadow. And so [*dio*, therefore] the child will be holy and will be called Son of God'" (Luke 1:35). I vindicate, too, the "ordinary" Christian who, in spite of the theologians, persists in believing that the Word was actually made flesh. I vindicate the expectation of the human race, pagan and Jewish, that dimly discerned that heroes, giants, or supermen would be born when the gods or the sons of God had dealings with the daughters of mortal men. Lastly, I relegate to the limbo of idle speculation one more theological myth, the myth that the Word could have taken flesh with or without the help of a human father, and that the human intellect can discern this fact.[14]

Let me indicate some special manifestations of Jesus' Word-consciousness, and throw into relief some possibly critical moments during his growth into full awareness of his mission and destiny.[15] First, I see him as a child in the temple, discoursing with the doctors (Luke 2:46–50).[16] I see him as in Leonardo's portrait, the light of divine wisdom already on his brow. The pure interpretation of the prophecies has been kept in the simple Jewish household, among the "poor of Yahweh," and already he astonishes those who should have been his teachers. He listens to them, and asks them questions; but they are amazed at his intelligence and his replies.

When he begins his public life, he soon proclaims that he is greater than Jonas or Solomon (Matt 12:38–42; Luke 11:29–32). He completes the Mosaic law in his own name, not, as Moses gave it, in the name of Yahweh (Matt 5:20–48). He moves through the world with the easy familiarity of a Son in his Father's house. Near Caesarea Philippi, by the Sea of Galilee, he asks his chosen disciples what they have to say of the Son of

---

14. Note that the constitutive role of the virgin birth for the incarnation, both physically and in the consciousness of Jesus, is the final answer of translation Christology to any charge or suspicion of adoptionism.

15. The "novel writing" mentioned in footnote 7 of this chapter starts here. But note that McIntyre in *Shape of Christology* points out that even those scholars who reject the possibility of any psychological study of Jesus—he mentions Barth, Bornkamm, Bultmann, and Käsemann—nevertheless "discuss attitudes, motives, ideas, reaction,s and even feelings of Jesus."

16. Schonfield draws attention to a similarity between this story and a story that Josephus tells about his own boyhood. *Passover Plot,* 47. But we should note the accuracy of the Lukan account of the Jewish travelling arrangements; and whatever else the author was doing, he was not writing a biography of Josephus! Note too that this story appears to come from a tradition that did not know of the virgin birth of Jesus.

Man. St. Peter produces his inspired confession: "You are the Christ, the Son of the living God" (Matt 16:16).[17] It is a moment of truth, a moment fraught with destiny. Jesus rises to the occasion, and implicitly confirms his natural divine Sonship. He says, "Simon son of Jonah, you are a happy man! Because it was not flesh and blood which revealed this to you but my Father in heaven" (Matt 16:17). In these two verses, 16 and 17, there is a clear parallelism between "Simon son of Jonah" and "Christ, the Son of the living God."[18]

In the periods spent in the desert, in the nights passed on the hillsides in communion with his Father, Jesus comes to an ever clearer knowledge of his mission and destiny. Greatness breaks over him in ever deeper insights followed by long periods of incubation, leading to conscious realization and acceptance of his destiny. In his arguments with the Pharisees, his thoughts about himself become more precise and more comprehensive. Every confrontation is a challenge to go either forward or backward, and there can be no going back. He is greater, even, than the father Abraham; indeed, before ever Abraham came to be, the proper name of Yahweh, I Am, is his by right of nature (John 8:58).[19]

His way is now clear before him. He is sure of himself now, as never before. He knows exactly where he is going, and he knows that no one will be able to stop him. As he goes up to Jerusalem to die, as he squares up to the passion, he feels the force of his moral goodness overflowing from him, and so he proclaims it to the world: "Come to me, all you who labor

---

17. Fenton, *Saint Matthew*, 266, thinks that Matthew here reflects the more developed faith of the early Christian community. Cullmann, *Christology*, 280-81, suggests that Matthew 16:16 has combined Mark 8:29 with John 6:69. But Butler, *Originality*, 132-33, showed the parallelism and Semitic content and rhythm of Matthew 16:13-23. Butler pointed out six contrasts in Matthew, all missing in Mark. I would add a seventh, between "Christ, the Son of the living God" and "Simon, son of Jonah," and I would contrast verses 16 and 17 in this way:

v. 16:
(i) *apokritheis de Simon Petros eipen*
(ii) *su ei ó Christos*
(iii) *óuios tou theou* zontos.

v. 17:
(i) *apokritheis de ó Iesous eipen auto*
(ii) *Makarios ei Simon*
(iii) *Bariona*.

18. See the previous note for the Greek text.

19. But see chapter 10, note 6 about such passages.

and are overburdened, and I will give you rest. Shoulder my yoke and learn from me, for I am gentle and humble in heart, and you will find rest for your souls. Yes, my yoke is easy and my burden light" (Matt 11:28–30).

At the Last Supper, Jesus reaches the plenitude of Word-consciousness and the fullness of sacrificial charity. He rises from the table and washes the feet of his disciples (John 13:4–11). He gives them his body to eat, and his blood to drink: the body in the state of having been delivered for us (*didomenon*, Luke 22:19); the blood in the state of having been shed for us (*ekkunnomenon*, Luke 22:20). He whose word is creative, in whom all things are created, speaks the creative words: "This is my body . . . This is . . . my blood." He has now finished the work that he set out to do. The passion will follow almost as a matter of course. He addresses his chosen disciples and, in the fullness of his Word-consciousness, he penetrates into the heart of that Trinity that he has never left.[20]

> To have seen me is to have seen the Father, . . .
> You must believe me when I say
> that I am in the Father and the Father is in me; . . .
> I shall ask the Father,
> and he will give you another Advocate
> to be with you forever, . . .
> the Advocate, the Holy Spirit,
> whom the Father will send in my name,
> will teach you everything
> and remind you of all I have said to you . . .
> when the Spirit of truth comes
> he will lead you to the complete truth . . .
> I have been telling you all this in metaphors,
> the hour is coming
> when I shall no longer speak to you in metaphors;
> but tell you about the Father in plain words. . . .
> I came from the Father and have come into the world
> and now I leave the world to go to the Father.
> (John 14:9, 11, 16, 26; 16:13, 25, 28)

It was at this point that the disciples said to him, "Now you are speaking plainly and not using metaphors: Now we see that you know

---

20. The Gospel of John chapters 14–16 are the Farewell Discourse, followed by a final Prayer in chapter 17. What I have said elsewhere about the Gospel of John applies even more thoroughly here. It is the interpretation of Jesus as the incarnate Son of God that I accept here, without claiming that Jesus said all the words attributed to him by the author of this Gospel.

everything, and do not have to wait for questions to be put into words; because of this we believe that you came from God" (John 16:29, 30).

Finally, Jesus lifts up his eyes to heaven and addresses the Father:

> Father, the hour has come:
> glorify your Son
> so that your Son may glorify you; . . .
> I have glorified you on earth
> and finished the work
> that you gave me to do.
> Now, Father, it is time for you to glorify me
> with that glory I had with you
> before ever the world was. . . .
> I pray not only for these,
> but for those also who through their words will believe in me.
> May they all be one.
> Father may they be one in us,
> as you are in me and I am in you,
> so that the world may believe it was you who sent me. . . .
> Father,
> I want those you have given me
> to be with me where I am,
> so that they may always see the glory
> you have given me
> because you loved me
> before the foundation of the world.
> (John 17:1, 4, 5, 20, 21, 24)[21]

There follows the passion, with its total darkness pierced by a final shaft of light.[22] His enemies have had their way. They have done all that it was possible for them to do to destroy him. But their worst efforts have been in vain. He passes through the jaws of death and rises from the tomb, immortal now and incorruptible.

The Christian has seen a vision of Joy in the heart of the morning. He has seen a young God rising from the tomb in the silent hours of the early morning, laying death low once and for all. The old gods are dead. Jupiter, Poseidon, Neptune, bearded octogenarians all, have passed

---

21. In using these passages as if they expressed the development of Jesus' thinking, I have to suppose that they have some basis in fact. I must therefore believe that the beloved disciple saw things about Jesus that others did not, and that this was the basis of these passages, which may stem from the Johannine school at Ephesus in about 90 CE.

22. See Appendix C for my theory of the resurrection of Jesus Christ.

away. In their place we have a young God, immortal with the freshness of eternal youth, victor over sin and death. In their place we have, at last, the complete expression of the incarnation realized in fact.

Until very recently, this Joy lingered on in our life and liturgy. It was present in the exultant peal of the *lapis revolutus est*; it was in the serene strains of the "Victimae Paschali." It found ecstatic expression in the *Resurrexit sicut dixit* of the "Regina Coeli." It is our firm conviction that this Joy will one day come to claim us for its own.

16

The Incarnation Fulfilled in History
The Cosmic Christ

The incarnation cannot be repeated. God, who spoke to us in many ways through the prophets, has revealed himself once and for all in his Son. The triune nature of the deity is too precise, too well-defined, to be the subject of other vague and incomplete revelations. One man has revealed the Trinity to us. That man is Jesus Christ. A misguided irenic spirit should never induce us to obscure that fact.[1] The incarnation is fulfilled in history by extension, and by realization or understanding. The extension occurs in and through the people of God, the mystical body of Christ. We are joined to Christ's humanity by faith and love and to that extent, no more and no less, we share in the incarnation. The hypostatic union is unique, and is not communicable. One man, and one man alone, exists as the Word expressed in human form. The share that we have in Christ's life is brought about by grace. This grace is a substantial, not a subsistential, modification to our nature; it is an elevation of our nature to a higher plane, the plane of God's intimate life. By grace we can know and love God in his Trinity of persons. We attain to the Trinity by faith in Christ. In the uncertainty of this life, that faith does not normally amount to vision.

In this book, I do not treat the subject of faith that becomes vision in another life. Likewise, I do not seek here to relate the church to the world and Christianity; to humanity or to Humanism; and to the other world religions. But I must nonetheless mention Teilhard de Chardin's inspiring vision of the Super-Christ who is Christ himself, expanding with the

1. But see chapter 8 note 5 for a mitigation of this stance.

The Incarnation Fulfilled in History

expansion of human consciousness, Christ the Omega Point of all our striving, the term and goal of our conscious evolution. "Christ-Omega: the Christ, therefore, who animates and gathers up all the biological and spiritual energies developed by the universe."[2]

One must link this splendid vision with the two hymns in Ephesians and Colossians. According to Ephesians, God plans to bring everything together under Christ as head (recapitulation, gathering up; Eph 1:10); while, according to Colossians, God wants all things to be reconciled through Christ and into Christ (*eis auton*, Col 1:20). This reconciliation after estrangement sounds a note that is not always clearly expressed in Teilhard's work; rather it is reconciliation into Christ, which can only mean the cosmic Christ, who is none other than Jesus of Nazareth. Teilhard's vision is continuous with that of St. Paul, for whom Christ the Lord of creation was none other than Christ crucified. According to St. Paul, God's plan is to put everything under Christ's feet, so that in the end Christ may hand the kingdom over to God the Father, and God will be all in all (1 Cor 15:24–28).

The incarnation is also fulfilled in history by understanding. The insights of Sts. Paul and John, Athanasius, Augustine, and Thomas Aquinas have helped considerably in bringing the church to an understanding of the meaning of the incarnation realized in Jesus Christ, the Head of the church. We may one day reach an expression of the doctrine that will be valid for time and for eternity. It is my hope that the theory offered in these pages will help toward the attainment of this goal.

---

2. Teilhard de Chardin, *Science*, 167.

Appendix A

A Note on Aristotelian and Scholastic Concepts

In chapter 6 I refer to the Aristotelian concepts of "substance" and "accident," and to their sixteenth century scholastic interpretations. It would be of value to add a few words here about these concepts and their relevance to the incarnation as understood by translation Christology.

Aristotle distinguished ten categories, the principal one being substance, that is, a thing that exists in itself and not in another thing (e.g., a man or a horse). The other nine categories were "accidents" or "attributes" of some substance. They are: quantity, quality, relation, where, when, position, having, doing, and undergoing in the sense of being affected.[1]

The Scholastics, largely following Aristotle, further distinguished created things into potency and act. Potency is a capacity needing to be actuated, whereas act is the actuality or realization of that potency. An example of potency and act was given by matter and form, where "matter" meant "prime matter," which was a pure potency, a capacity to become any material object if actuated by the appropriate "act" or "form." A key example of matter and form for the Scholastics was the human body and soul, the soul being considered to be the "form" of the body. (Clearly in this context "form" means much more than "shape," though the Aristotelian concept of "form" may have originated from that idea.)

A more fundamental instance of potency and act is the pair essence and existence, where essence means what a thing is, and existence means the "act" by which it is. All created things were considered to be composed of essence and existence (i.e., potency and act). God alone was pure

---

1. Aristotle, *Categories*, 5.

Appendix A

Act. In him essence and existence were one. God was referred to by the Scholastics as *ipsum esse subsistens*, the pure subsistent act of existence.

I have criticized the Scholastic interpretation of Aristotle's categories because the Scholastics considered that substances and their "accidents" were distinct realities, which could even be separated (notoriously in Thomistic "transubstantiation"). I contend that such concepts as "substance" and "accident" are distinctions made by the mind; that a tree, for example, cannot be separated from its "quantity" (or height, or weight), but is conveniently thought to possess such an attribute. For a more accurate analysis of the material world, I would refer to modern physics with its subatomic particles, and not to such categories as Aristotle's "substance" and "accident."

RELEVANCE TO THE INCARNATION

The Scholastic categories of potency and act were subsequently used by Christian thinkers to interpret the incarnation. In his treatise on the incarnation in the *Summa Theologiae*, St. Thomas Aquinas held that there is only one *esse* (i.e., existence) in Christ.[2] Thus Christ's human nature, according to St. Thomas, is directly actuated by the divine existence, and in this way is joined to the Second Person of the Trinity, the eternal Son of God. Thus Aquinas held that there was just one person in Christ, the Second Person of the Trinity, who had assumed a human nature and thus possessed two natures, one divine and one human.

It is worth noting that no one has explained how a human nature could be actuated by the divine existence so as to "belong" to one person of the Trinity. In this regard, John Hick appears to be entirely justified in his contention that the formula of the Council of Chalcedon (that in Jesus Christ there is one divine person with two natures, divine and human) has never been successfully explained.[3]

Translation Christology avoids this problem by maintaining that in Jesus Christ the eternal Word of God was translated into human form. Against translation Christology, it can be argued that there is no true incarnation here because a translation of the Word is not the Word himself. While this objection may be valid as far as the defense of the Council of Chalcedon's formula goes, it remains true that translation Christology

2. Aquinas, *Summa* 3, 17, 2.
3. Hick, *Metaphor*, 1–14, especially 12.

starts from the incarnation described in John 1:14, where we are told that the Word was made flesh. Indeed translation Christology fits this phrase far better than an assumption Christology of the sort favored by the Scholastics. In addition, translation Christology explains the Johannine phrase in terms of the Epistle 1 John 1:1–4, where we are told that the invisible has become visible, the inaudible has become audible, and the intangible has become tangible. Indeed, translation Christology derives an understanding of incarnation directly from the sources. Moreover, translation Christology safeguards the blessed Trinity. Unlike John Hick, who seems to doubt the reality of the Trinity, I maintain that the eternal Son or Word of God was translated into human form in Jesus Christ. Likewise, translation Christology maintains the full humanity of Christ with no shadow of Docetism (the theory that Christ only appeared to have a human nature and was simply God masquerading as a man). Out of deference to the tradition proclaimed by Chalcedon, I do not call Jesus a human person. But I maintain that he lacks nothing that is required for human personality. Jesus Christ translates the eternal Word for us and is indeed the Word expressed in human form.

Appendix B

The Impassibility of God
A Critique

In this appendix I intend to examine the defects in a rigidly Scholastic notion of an absolutely immutable and impassible deity, and determine what, if anything, can be learned from the incarnation.

The God of Scholasticism was simply identical, in the Christian faith, with the God of Abraham, the Father of Jesus. But this God was sadly misconceived. Let us listen to Karl Rahner here:

> For it is true, come what may, and a dogma, that the Logos himself has become man: thus that he himself has become something that he had not always been (*formaliter*); and therefore that what has so become is, as just itself and of itself, God's reality. Now if this is a truth of faith, ontology must allow itself to be guided by it (as in analogous instances in the doctrine of the Trinity), must seek enlightenment from it, and grant that while God remains immutable "in himself," he can come to be "in the other," and that *both* assertions must really and truly be made of the same God as God.[1]

Rahner immediately notes that this ability of God to come to be in the other cannot be restricted to the incarnation. At least, he raises the question whether it might be "necessary to go back to a *more general* theory of the relationship between God and his world, of which the relationship 'Logos-human nature' would appear as a special case."[2]

The need to modify the rigid structure of traditional theism was seen by von Hügel and by Paul Tillich, among others. Baron von Hügel,

---

1. Rahner, *Theological*, vol. 1, 181, note 3.
2. Ibid., 183; also vol. 4, 113–14, note 3.

The Impassibility of God

after Krause, used the term "panentheism," which has also been used by Hartshorne and Rahner and adopted, in his own curious equivocal way, by John A. T. Robinson.[3] For my part, I am not very much concerned about labels. I wish to investigate the reality of God's relationship to the world which he has made.

I note Tillich's main objection to theological theism. "God as a subject makes me into an object which is nothing more than an object. He deprives me of my subjectivity because he is all-powerful and all-knowing."[4] And again: "This is the God Nietzsche said had to be killed because nobody can tolerate being made into a mere object of absolute knowledge and absolute control. This is the deepest root of atheism."[5]

In order to meet Tillich's objection, it is necessary to explore the subjectivity of God by the only way open to us, the way of analogy, or affirmation coupled with negation (*via negativa*), in order to glimpse the possibility of a higher synthesis. But first let me say why we need to believe that God and the world are distinct, and why we need to believe that God and the world are one.

The subjective basis of theism lies in man's need to live forever. Objective bases of theism exist, in philosophy and, especially, in the study of Christian origins; but I am not concerned with those here but with a particular subjective basis of theism namely man's need to live forever. I am aware that God brought the Hebrew people to a knowledge of himself long before the Hebrew people came to believe in life after death. But I am concerned here with myself, and with modern man. Suffice it to say that if I could believe in an immortal soul, immortal in its own right, independently of the body, I might be able to bypass the ultimate, final, inescapable need for God. Similarly, if I could believe in absolute, secure immortality for our race on this or other planets, then I might be able to bypass the need for God. But the progress of human knowledge shows ever more clearly that, for all of us living now and for most or all of our descendants, there is no real hope for our ultimate survival except in God, a God who is powerful enough to work a cosmic miracle.[6]

---

3. Robinson, *Exploration*, 83; Rahner, *Concise Theological Dictionary*, s.v. "Panentheism"; *DzS*, 3001 (1782).

4. Tillich, *Courage*, 179.

5. Ibid., 179.

6. Note that in the consciousness of the deceased, a general resurrection would follow immediately on his or her death, even if he or she was dead for a trillion years or more.

Appendix B

Let me note that the desire for eternal (that is, unending) life is not purely selfish; rather, such a desire is ultimately involved with concern to live a life of ultimate (that is, unending) meaning, purpose, and moral value. To the theist, life without God would be finally meaningless. In prospect, it would gather up to a single point of meaninglessness at death; and this point would cast its meaningless and empty shadow back over the whole of life. Either death is a beginning, or human life is ultimately pointless.[7]

Second, the subjective basis of pantheism lies in the need to value the world, including oneself and one's fellow men, truly, ultimately, not merely as second class beings. This even involves a real (but dangerous) desire to worship the world, and also to find ultimate meaning and value in the current instant. An objective basis of pantheism lies in some of the great non-Christian religions, and in the unanimous witness of the Christian mystics.

I wish to grasp the nettle here, and to consider what the relationship between God and the world must be, and what it cannot be, from God's side. I begin from a fact of experience, namely, the I-Thou relationship that we experience with other human beings. We cannot get inside other minds to know with their knowledge, feel with their feeling. So complete is our isolation, in spite of the most intimate, even lifelong friendship, that it is true to say that there is no purely theoretical refutation of solipsism (the theory that I alone exist and that all else is part of my mental equipment). In order to refute solipsism, we have to be practical or witty, preferably both. One thinks of Bertrand Russell's story about the woman who wrote to him saying that she found solipsism such an attractive theory that she was surprised more people did not hold it! But that is by the way. As a normal, ineluctable fact of human experience, the I-Thou relationship is established—always provided, of course, we do not lapse into solipsism!

We easily extend the I-Thou relationship to our acquaintance with the deity. We objectify God, and he remains behind the veil as the Other. If in mystical experience we seem to pierce the veil, this only serves to emphasize the existence of that veil throughout the normal course of our lives.

---

7. I would not hold that for the atheist life has no meaning. I would say that for the atheist life has no ultimate meaning, i.e., no meaning that extends through death and into eternity.

The Impassibility of God

Now let us "project" imaginatively; let us try to visualize this relationship from the other side, from God's side. The condition of being "shut off" from the other as other is surely sourced from the very essence of finitude. Such a condition implies boundaries, limits to the self. It is unthinkable that God should have this experience. It follows that God does not know the other as other. It also follows that the other is not present to God as other. It follows indeed that God is identical with whatever he creates, from his side at least; he quite literally puts himself into his work. We cannot visualize or imagine this, except conceptually, by way of negation (*via negativa*). But it seems that from God's side the identity is complete.

Yet the distinction quite clearly exists, from our side at least. Have we reached a contradiction? I think not. In order to show why not, it will be necessary to examine the properties of the metaphysical relationship of identity, and I shall do this by first considering the analogous properties of the mathematical relationship of equality.

Mathematical equality is usually regarded as an equivalence relation,[8] having the properties of being reflexive, symmetric, and transitive. Thus, if equality is defined on a set S, we have:

a. If a is any element of S, then a equals a.
b. If a and b are elements of S, and if a equals b, then b equals a.
c. If a, b, and c are elements of S, and if a equals b and b equals c, then a equals c.

Of course, (b) and (c), under suitable axioms of substitutivity, imply that if a, b, and c are elements of S, and if a equals c and b equals c, then a equals b: things that are equal to the same thing are equal to each other.

Metaphysical identity has analogous properties: it is reflexive, symmetric, and transitive:

a. For every thing a, a is a.
b. For all things a and b, if a is b then b is a.
c. For all things a, b, and c, if a is b and b is c then a is c.

Here (a) is the principle of identity or law of contradiction, which affirms the reflexive character of the relationship of identity,[9] and which admits of absolutely no exception, with all due respect to Hegel and oth-

---

8. Mirsky, *Introduction*, 186.
9. In *Being and Becoming*, Hawkins holds (wrongly, I now think) that the principle of identity affirms the symmetry of the relation of otherness, 164.

ers. If an angel from heaven preached against the principle of identity, we would have to declare him anathema. If the doctrine of the Trinity were a contradiction, it would be so much the worse for the doctrine of the Trinity.[10]

Again, (b) and (c) yield the principle of comparative identity: two things that are identical with the same third thing are identical with each other. This principle holds absolutely, in the created order; but it does not apply to the relations between the persons and the divine essence in God. The Father is God, and the Son is God, the unique and self-same God; but the Father is not the Son. This exception is part of the unique mystery of the Trinity (probably the least interesting part, from a moral and spiritual point of view): it has no parallel, even remote, in the created order.

I now suggest that the Christian doctrine of creation, properly conceived (properly but imperfectly and inadequately, of course), implies an exception to the symmetric nature of the relationship of identity. That is, as St. Thomas Aquinas said, the Creator-creature relationship is asymmetric. But it is asymmetric in a way beyond what St. Thomas saw during his working life.[11] While the world, from its side, is clearly not identical with God, yet God, from his side, is identical not only with himself, but also, in a unique way, with the world that he creates as well. Again, this mystery is without parallel in the created order. It is also the foundation of the possibility of the incarnation, just as the total divine transcendence is the foundation of the total divine immanence.

I have used mathematics to illustrate my metaphysics. Mathematicians and metaphysicians may wish to know whether I am here defending a strict isomorphism or simply an analogy.[12] The point is an academic one that concerns the relationship between modern mathematics and traditional metaphysics. On the one hand, I would agree with the moderns that the old hierarchy of the degrees of abstraction, still defended by Jacques Maritain in "Les Degres du Savoir,"[13] has broken down, and that modern mathematics is as abstract as traditional metaphysics ever was.[14]

---

10. For a discussion of the law of contradiction from the point of view of scientific positivism, see Quine, "Meaning and Translation," 162–65.

11. For example, see Chesterton's *St. Thomas Aquinas*.

12. A mathematical isomorphism obtains between sets which have exactly the same structure.

13. Maritain, *Degrees*, 38–46.

14. Fraenkel, *Abstract*, Ch. 1, especially 12–13.

The Impassibility of God

On the other hand, I do not accept that Bertrand Russell's attempted reduction of mathematics to formal logic has been entirely successful, or that the element of intuition can be completely excluded from mathematical discourse.[15] But the main point here is that I believe that those properties which hold for the relationship of equality in mathematics, namely reflexiveness, symmetry, and transitivity, hold also for the relationship of identity in metaphysics. Apart from the two exceptions stated previously, metaphysical identity is reflexive, symmetric, and transitive.

There are two immediate consequences of this theory, the first as regards the divine immutability, and the second as regards the divine impassibility as maintained by traditional thought. As regards immutability, I can still accept Rahner's claim that God is immutable in himself, *immutabilis in se*. In fact, there is a sense in which this belief is absolutely essential to a sound philosophy or theology. God holds the whole world in his power; as Mother Julian of Norwich said, it is a small thing but he loves it. Moreover, this love is invincible, a fact shown most clearly in the word "friend" addressed by Jesus to Judas at the moment of betrayal (Matt 26:50). His love could not be invincible if his power were not invincible. The immutability of God in himself simply means that nothing can be added to or subtracted from the totality of being. To deny this is to lapse into absurdity.

On the other hand, I agree with Rahner that God is mutable in the other, *mutabilis in alio*, and that this truth is involved in both the creation and the incarnation. (See footnotes 1 and 2 above.) But, following my previous analysis, I would add an important qualification: God is changeable in the other, but not as other (*mutabilis in alio, sed non ut alio*). By this distinction I mean to highlight the fundamental point that the "otherness" exists only from the side of the creature, not from God's side.

It follows that when the creature changes, God too changes, inasmuch as and in so far as he is identical, from his side of the Creator-creature relationship, with that which he creates. The justification for maintaining the assertion that God is immutable in himself lies in the fact that the change that he undergoes in the other (but not as other) does not, as it were, undermine the basic stability of his Being. He is in no danger of being swept away by events, hopelessly entangled in an uncontrollable cosmic process. I recall the words of Wisdom 7:27: "Although alone, she

---

15. Poincaré, "Mathematical Creation," 14–17.

Appendix B

[God's Wisdom] can do all; herself unchanging, she makes all things new. In each generation she passes into holy souls, she makes them friends of God and prophets."

And also those of Romans 14:4, "he will stand, you may be sure, because the Lord has power to make him stand."

Finally, at the term of this analysis, I adopt a very different standpoint from the traditional one as regards divine impassibility. I would not now concede that God is impassible in any sense at all. Indeed, if "suffer" were to be identified with the Scholastic category of *pati*, and if this in turn were equated with "transition from potency to act," *transire de potentia in actum*, then one would have to say that God could not suffer. But I reject this use of the word altogether. To suffer means to experience pain or grief. For God to suffer means to take all the suffering of the world into himself, to have already taken it into himself before it comes to be, so that when any creature suffers, God too suffers. Indeed the distinction between God and the creature from the creature's side allows imperfection in its suffering; the identity from God's side allows none in his. Thus, when any creature suffers, God too suffers, more, not less, than the creature does.[16]

Thus I find insufficient the position adopted by the late Professor Mascall in defending God's impassibility in "Existence and Analogy."[17] Dr. Mascall objected to the view that swamps God's compassion with his interior beatitude: "If I am plagued with a raging toothache it will not comfort me much to be told that someone whose tooth is equally bad is finding it quite bearable because he has just been left an immense fortune."[18] I find this objection quite unanswerable, and that is why I defend God's invincibility but not his impassibility. I believe that a God who could not really get involved with his world would not have bothered to create it in the first place.

Here I wish to quote from William Temple: "All those who have such experience of fellowship with God as commends itself to the conscience of other men as genuine, agree in depicting God as at once exalted above all the tumult and anxiety of life, and also suffering grief and indignation at the conduct of man." Dr. Temple quoted Isaiah 57:15–17 and 5:3, 4

16. Dostoyevsky, *Crime*, 380: "the whole of human suffering."

17. Mascall, *Existence*, 134–43.

18. Ibid., 142. On pp. 142–43 Dr. Mascall vindicated for God a compassion that now seems to me more notional than real.

The Impassibility of God

in support.[19] Of course, God suffers uniquely and terribly in the passion of Christ, in a special way far beyond what I am defending here; but the suffering of Christ in its turn serves to show us that in any suffering it is God who suffers most.

This fact throws into stark relief the horror of man's inhumanity to man. I quote here from Robert Castle's *Litany from the Underground*, 1 and 2:

> O God, who lives in tenements, who goes to segregated schools, who is beaten in precincts, who is unemployed, Help us to know you."[20]
>
> O God, whose black body is twisted still in death in some rice paddy, for free elections in Vietnam, and swinging softly from some tree in the United States because he went to vote in a free election,
>
> Help us to change our sick society.[21]
> Minister: O God, I see you,
> People: O God, you're crying,
> Minister: O God, you're wounded,
> People: O God, you're bleeding,
> Minister: O God, you're dying,
> People: O God, you're dead.
> Minister: Long live God!
> People: Long live God![22]

I add a word here on Dietrich Bonhoeffer's teaching about the world coming of age. I think that this is essentially true, although there must always be something relative and arbitrary about a coming of age. No doubt a thousand years from now men, if they still exist, will consider us to have been very immature. But I would agree that man's coming of age means some sort of "self-denying ordinance" of God as Sovereign Ruler and Supreme Being, and I would say that man comes of age precisely because God, like a wise parent, insists that man must mature properly and stand on his own two feet.

There is a parable for this event, I think, in the history of the Jewish people. When the elders of Israel asked Samuel to give them a king to

---

19. Temple, *Christus*, 96.
20. Castle, "Litany," 1, 63.
21. Castle, "Litany," 2, 154.
22. Ibid., 2, 158.

Appendix B

rule over them, like the other nations, Yahweh saw to it that they were solemnly warned of the consequences:

> These will be the rights of the king who is to reign over you. He will take your sons and assign them to his chariotry and cavalry, and they will run in front of his chariot. He will use them as leaders of a thousand and leaders of fifty; he will make them plough his ploughland and harvest his harvest and make his weapons of war and the gear for his chariots. He will also take your daughters as perfumers, cooks and bakers. He will take the best of your fields, of your vineyards and olive groves and give them to his officials. He will tithe your crops and vineyards to provide for his eunuchs and his officials. He will take the best of your manservants and maidservants, of your cattle and your donkeys, and make them work for him. He will tithe your flocks, and you yourselves will become his slaves. When that day comes, you will cry out on account of the king you have chosen for yourselves, but on that day God will not answer you. (1 Sam 8:10–18)

But of course the people insisted on having a king. Likewise there are still those among us who insist on seeing in revelation the story of God's sovereignty. I think that this is a mistake. The story of revelation is, I think, the story of God's self-communication in love. There is the divine self-communication within the Trinity, and the further self-communication in creation. I am reminded of the fine phrase by Christian Duquoc who says that revelation, in both Testaments, shows us a God in love with man, not with power and glory.[23] Even St. Thomas Aquinas, who believed firmly in the glory of God, taught that God seeks his glory not for his sake but for ours.[24]

The tendency to make God into a Sovereign Ruler or Supreme Being holds for us the same sort of unfortunate consequences as does the desire for an earthly king. We could well project the passage from the First Book of Samuel quoted above, and imagine God saying to the human race:

> If you make me your Sovereign King and Dictator, you will fight wars in my name; you will kill and starve and torture in order to vindicate my honor, until everyone who kills his brother will think that he is doing me a favor. So our opponents may well say, as

---

23. Duquoc, *Christologie*, 333: "*Dieu est passioné pour l'homme . . . pas pour la puissance et la gloire.*"

24. Aquinas, *Summa* 2-2, 132, 1, ad 1: "*Deus suam gloriam non quaerit propter se, sed propter nos.*"

some have previously done: "Your God is on our side!" but still the slaughter will go on. And all this because you could not see that I wanted to love you, not to rule you; I wished not to be your Sovereign but your Lover; you would not open yourself to the devastating onslaught of Love.

Of course, it is one thing to diagnose the disease; it is quite another to cure it. Love makes demands far in advance of those generally made by rulers. "Yes, love is a fire no waters avail to quench, no floods to drown; for love, a man will give up all that he has in the world, and think nothing of his loss." (Song of Songs 8:7, Ronald Knox translation).

The sense in which I have defended identity between God and his creation is transcended in the incarnation, where the identity exists from both sides. Also, as the pioneering work of Karl Rahner indicated, this critique of the impassibility of God has only been possible on the basis of what the incarnation revealed to us about the divine nature.

Appendix C

The Resurrection of Jesus Christ

On June 7, 1974, I published an article in the Catholic Herald on the subject of the resurrection of Jesus Christ. That article relied on the Shroud of Turin, which was believed at that time to be the authentic burial cloth of Jesus Christ. It is necessary to reconsider the article in the light of the carbon-dating tests carried out on the shroud in 1988.

My article suggested that the resurrection of Jesus Christ was an irreversible "gymnastic" conquest of the forces of catabolism (i.e., biological destruction). According to this theory, the passion of Jesus served as a physical and psychological catharsis or purification of the organism, in which the principle of death and decay was destroyed. Jesus therefore rose from the tomb immortal and incorruptible. Perhaps I had better say something about the theoretical basis of this theory before I consider such facts as are available to support it.

It is often assumed that death is natural to man, and inevitable. Death is certainly a natural event, but there is no theoretical proof of its inevitability. A tree can live for hundreds of years. It manages to do this by restricting its needs to the biological minimum, and sacrificing much in the way of possible evolutionary development. It puts down deep roots, and specializes in a thick protective covering or bark, so that short of destruction by lightning or tempest, it has little to fear from its natural enemies. Now the vertebrates, including man, are not in this comfortable situation. The vertebrates have sacrificed security for the sake of progress. Their basic structure consists of a rather fragile skeleton of articulated bones. Their needs are many and complicated; the risks they run are legion. If a vertebrate is to survive, it is required to show much more ingenuity than does a tree. Because of the parallelism of natural development, the vertebrates are, by and large, endowed with more ingenuity than trees. It may well turn out, in the long run, that the vertebrates are able to achieve a measure of survival far in excess of that enjoyed by trees.

The span of human life is increasing with the progress of medical science. It is not yet true to say that the conquest of disease is in sight. Some diseases, like cancer, still defy medical skill. But it is not simply the utopian sentiment to hope that one day these diseases will be conquered by science. There remains the larger problem of senility and death.

Senility seems to be inevitable. The course of human life appears to be clearly mapped: we grow up, we hold our own for a little while, and then we break up. One reason for this seeming inevitability is that the same forces that build us up also serve to break us up. The energy used in digesting our food takes its toll on our organism. Eventually the balance declines irreversibly on the side of destruction and decay.[1]

In technical language, the biological processes by which we grow up and break up are called metabolism. There is constructive metabolism, by which nutritive material is built up into living matter; and destructive metabolism, also called catabolism, by which protoplasm, the basic substance of life in plants and animals, is broken down into simpler substances. In the early phase of our life the forces of constructive metabolism have the upper hand. Later, when we reach maturity, a kind of balance is achieved. Finally, when we begin to grow old, the forces of catabolism come into their own and achieve their final triumph in the death and destruction of the organism.

Now there is no theoretical reason why the balance between the forces of constructive metabolism and the forces of catabolism, which exists, more or less, during the years of maturity, should not be maintained indefinitely. To achieve this end it would be necessary to find some way of destroying the efficacy of the forces of catabolism. This might also involve the cessation of metabolism. It might mean, not a continued balance of warring forces, but a permanent truce. The achievement of immortality might well mean that biological processes had ceased. In that case the immortal person would be in a state which was biologically static, leaving the full psychological dynamism of his or her personality to unfold and progress indefinitely. That is the kind of thing I think happened in the passion and resurrection of Christ.

1. Note that we are perhaps genetically programmed to grow old and die. Once again genetics may hold the key to one of life's ultimate mysteries.

Appendix C

The factual evidence to support this theory is very slight. The Gospel record of the passion and resurrection of Jesus gives us few details of his physical state during the time he spent in the tomb. But there is another record that came into prominence during the twentieth century and which is of a surprisingly scientific kind. I refer to the Shroud of Turin, venerated as the winding-sheet in which the body of Jesus was wrapped for burial.

The shroud is unique among relics, for when it first began to attract the attention of intellectuals its authenticity was strongly attacked by Catholic priests and defended by agnostics in the French Academy. The history of the dispute can be read in any one of a number of works on the subject, and I shall not recapitulate it here.[2] Neither shall I describe in detail the imprints on the shroud, or repeat the strong evidence that the man who was laid in the shroud was Jesus Christ.

One point does need to be explained. In 1988 the Shroud of Turin was submitted to carbon-dating tests. The test results were unanimous in dating the shroud to the fourteenth century CE. The basic point that needs to be made here is that if the carbon-dating results are right, then the Shroud of Turin is a copy of an original, which was most probably destroyed.[3] As a copy, the shroud contains the information that was present on the original, just as a copy of the New Testament contains the information which was present in the original manuscripts. For my purposes, whether the shroud is an original or a copy is almost irrelevant.

The shroud seems to show that Jesus was medically dead when he was laid in the tomb. It appears that rigor mortis had set in, apparently at once. Even more conclusive for some experts is the evidence of post-mortem bleeding, an exudation of serous fluid with clotted blood in the middle. Hematologists assure us that this is quite different from the stains left by blood that flows during the life of the victim.

This interpretation was challenged by John Reban, who claimed that the victim was alive when laid in the shroud.[4] The question of medical death is not strictly relevant to the theory I am proposing. The death of Jesus has a symbolic value in Christian theology. It is the supreme

---

2. See, for instance, Rinaldi, *The Man in the Shroud*.

3. For example, Currer-Briggs, *Shroud Mafia*. Note too that Ian Wilson, in *The Blood*, 219–31, held that the carbon-dating tests may have been skewed by the presence of a bacterial or "bioplastic" coating on the shroud.

4. Cf. John Reban's *Inquest*.

sacrifice, by which mankind was dedicated to God in Christ, sanctified in principle according to the literal meaning of the word sacrifice (i.e., *sacrum facere*, to make holy or sacred). It is possible that, as Reban suggested, theological and not medical death would suffice for this. It is also difficult to see how medical death can be reconciled in modern terms with the complete absence of corruption.

But what is important from the practical point of view is the conquest of the principle of death and decay, the achievement of immortal and incorruptible life. Let us suppose, for the sake of argument, that Jesus was dead in the technical or medical sense. I am going to suggest that during the thirty or so hours he spent in the tomb he returned to life.

First, let us examine the state of Jesus' body at the time of burial, on the double assumption that the shroud, or its original, definitely belonged to Jesus and that the imprints reflect the state of his body when buried. (Throughout the remainder of this article, the word "shroud" will mostly refer to the original winding-sheet, which may not be identical with the Shroud of Turin.) No bones were broken. The nails through the hands passed through Destot's space where the hand joins the wrist. The single nail which fixed the feet went through the second metatarsal space, immediately under Lisfranc's joint.[5] The loss of blood was comparatively small. The spear which pierced the side of Jesus went between the fifth and sixth ribs. There is a dispute as to whether it entered the right praecordia of the heart or missed both heart and aorta, affecting only the lungs.

The scourging was done with the flagrum not the flagellum. The flagrum consisted of long, thin thongs with weighted ends, which left deep bruises in the form of dumbbells over most of the body. The crown, or rather cap, of thorns would seem to have pierced veins and arteries, without greatly tearing their walls. The face had received a variety of modifications to the skin, from blows and perhaps scourging: bruises, excoriations, contusions, and open wounds. There are other wounds on the back and shoulders apparently caused by the carrying of the cross.

It is clear that no ordinary man would have recovered very quickly from this treatment, much less achieved immortality by undergoing it. But Jesus was not an ordinary man. The dignity with which he addressed Pilate after he had been scourged and crowned with thorns shows this. (I am assuming that this dialogue, however much it has had to be recon-

---

5. A recent archaeological discovery shows that in crucifixion the Romans used a single nail through the heels to fix the feet. This corresponds to a bloodstain on the shroud.

Appendix C

structed, has some basis in fact; the onus is on the critical scholar to prove the opposite if he can). I shall come presently to the psychological factors involved in my theory. These carry by far the most weight. I shall first mention two very slight indications that there may be a physical basis for the theory.

The body of Jesus was wrapped in the burial linen along with preservative spices, a mixture of myrrh and medicinal aloes. Thus the means were present for preventing the beginnings of decay while the recuperative forces of the organism went to work. Some of the direct stains on the shroud were caused, it seems, when blood already clotted on the body was redissolved and transferred to the cloth. This could have been the beginning of the physical process of recovery. All this amounts to very little and, as I have said, I place the major weight of the theory on psychological considerations.

It should be mentioned that the photographically negative stains on the shroud may have been formed by vaporography or by oxidation, and that neither of these processes involves decomposition. According to the first theory, the urea from febrile sweat formed ammoniac vapor, which reacted with the aloes and sensitized the cloth. The theory of oxidation obtained some support from experiments carried out by Dr. Judica. However, much study has now been done and many theories proposed. So far as I know, no definite theory has explained the origin of the images.

I come now to the psychological factors involved in the passion, death, and resurrection of Jesus. I do not wish to isolate these factors from the unique work that God performed in the incarnation of his Son, from the unique genetic composition of Jesus and its connection with his conception by the Holy Spirit in the womb of the Virgin Mary.[6]

There is a lot of evidence in the Gospels that Jesus foretold his death and resurrection. Some critical scholars have argued that he may have expected to be vindicated on the cross itself. But a more balanced view of the Gospel evidence is that, in the final days at least, the dominant conviction of his life was that he would die and on the third day rise again.

The shroud confirms that Jesus had a magnificent physique. This is already clear from his conduct during his trial, after the scourging. Moreover Pilate, who must have been a shrewd judge of men, was surprised to hear that he was already dead. I have mentioned already that,

---

6. Brown, *Birth*, 517–31.

The Resurrection of Jesus Christ

even if the shroud confirms death (in some sense) it shows no sign of irreparable damage to the organism. For practical purposes, then, in the design of God, Jesus may be considered to have been in a deep coma, a coma into which he entered with the dominating conviction that it was not the end. I should mention that there are some indications from the shroud that death may have been caused by spasms and slow asphyxiation caused by immobilization.

We can visualize Jesus, prepared for his ordeal by a life of physical rigor spent partly in desert fasts and night vigils on the hillsides; meeting the final revulsion by an agony in which his sweat became like drops of blood, as the author of Luke (or whoever wrote the two verses Luke 22:43–44) tells us;[7] undergoing the atrocious torture of crucifixion and its accompaniments but mastering his sufferings as the Gospel accounts indicate; finally feeling the darkness of death close in upon him. At that moment, his whole life and destiny were at stake. Despair gripped his spirit, and he cried out, "My God, my God, why have you deserted me?"

These words form the opening sentence of the 22nd Psalm. This psalm concludes on a note of triumph. It contains the statement that all the nations of the world will bow down before the Lord. The Gospels show that Jesus was very familiar with the psalms and quoted them freely. It seems that his very cry to God in despair brought his mind back to the thought of his eventual triumph. His conviction of his destiny, which normally had the clarity of vision, reasserted itself. He rallied his sinking spirits and, with all the energy of his being, cried out, "Father, into thy hands I commend my spirit."

That cry caused the tough centurion to exclaim, "This was indeed a son of God!" This was the most beautiful moment of history, the moment that is fixed forever in the Mass. Jesus commended his spirit into the hands of his Father. He knew that it was safe in those loving hands, and his trust was not disappointed. This tremendous act of loving confidence carried him through the jaws of death itself. Dominating his consciousness at this moment was the conviction that he would rise again. He died in the fullness of that conviction, and on the strength of that conviction he rose from the dead on the third day.

It is impossible to say exactly what happened in the darkness of the tomb. Perhaps there is a slight hint for us in the serenity of the face

---

7. Harrington, *Meeting*, 88.

Appendix C

depicted on the negative of the Shroud of Turin, dead but not defeated, bruised and battered but secretly triumphant. I would suggest that the dying conviction of Jesus remained deep in his mind to emerge at the appointed time as surely as if he had only slept. He had trusted his Father, and his Father repaid that trust. He had gambled with his life and won. He had tried the impossible and succeeded better, perhaps, than he knew and in a way in which he may not have expected to succeed. He emerged from the tomb, immortal and incorruptible.

I should make it clear that I do not rule out divine intervention here. I am in no way stubbornly opposed to the possibility of miracle. What I am anxious to maintain is that in the passion of Jesus, death was conquered physically as well as spiritually. In other words, the gymnastic aspect of the event was crucial.

I do not expect that this theory can be proved. The progress of science may throw some light on it or refute it, but it is not likely to prove its truth. It is offered for the consideration of the specialists, who may very well reject it out of hand. As far as I know, no doctor has seen a patient recover after rigor mortis had set in. But no doctor has had the privilege of examining a patient endowed as Jesus was with the hypostatic union and (finally at least) the beatific vision. Besides, the photographic evidence does not distinguish clearly between rigor mortis and muscular cramp caused by several hours on the cross.

I wish to mention a secondary point connected with the resurrection and to indicate some consequences of this theory.

The powers of the risen Christ remain rather obscure because we do not know the limits, if any, of the power of mind over matter, nor can we see a clear line where matter ends and spirit begins. It is clear that the unique powers of Jesus remained with him and were greatly enhanced. It was presumably by means of these powers that he ascended out of sight of the apostles. There his human history ends. He is now to be found in the suffering neighbor, in table fellowship, and in the enemy's brutal sneer.

One consequence of this theory is to refute entirely that cult of suffering that has been such a bad feature of much Christian piety. The sufferings of Jesus had a definite physical purpose, namely the purification of the organism and the attainment of immortal life. (Note the aptness, in this connection, of John 16:21.) It is true that our suffering may benefit our fellow men enormously even if it destroys us individually, but the cult of suffering for its own sake is morbid and mistaken.[8]

The passion remains Jesus' greatest manifestation of love toward man. He loved us better than some theologians will allow, for he gave his soul to death amid total darkness, trusting to his Father to vindicate his sacrifice. (As St. Paul told us, this was first and foremost the Father's own sacrifice; cf. Rom 8:32). He loved us to better purpose than the rationalist will allow, for by dying he achieved not only fame but personal fulfillment as well. It was no masochistic urge that bade him to pin himself to the cross, but obediential love; and by dying and rising again he showed us Who and What he was. He also destroyed death in principle, and ensured that death would be simply one episode in the total life of a true believer, not an end but a beginning, not a plunge into endless night but the dawn of a new and brighter day.

---

8. Young, "Incarnation," 103: "Thus the cross becomes a dramatic presentation of the fact that the way to overcome evil is not to escape from it, but to bear it creatively in the presence and power of God."

Appendix D

Toward a Modern Theory of the Holy Trinity

Trinitarian theology has become especially problematic in recent years.[1] A tendency toward some form of Sabellian modalism has reasserted itself,[2] with the emphasis being placed on the "economic" Trinity (the three aspects of God's work in history as Creator, Redeemer, and Sanctifier) rather than on the "immanent" Trinity (the eternally distinct persons, Father, Son, and Holy Spirit). From an exclusive emphasis on the economic Trinity it seems a short step to deny or suspend judgment about the existence of the immanent Trinity altogether. This can easily be done in the name of good ecumenical or interfaith relations. It can be felt that the Jews, for instance, may come to accept the economic Trinity as one of the facts of history, while the doctrine of the immanent Trinity must remain forever at variance with the absolute unity of God conceived as the fundamental principle of Jewish religion.

Whatever the value of this modern trend, the theory expounded here follows on from the traditional doctrine of the "immanent" Trinity expounded by theologians like St. Augustine and St. Thomas Aquinas in the West (and in the East most notably by the Cappadocian Fathers). My theory seeks to develop the doctrine in the light of a modern understand-

---

1. This appendix first appeared as an article in *Christian Renewal*, a publication of Roderick Bell's, in No. 6, Summer 1972, 14–16. It has been slightly modified here and some references to recent theology have been added.

2. Sabellius was condemned as a heretic for teaching that the Father, the Son, and the Holy Spirit are in fact one and the same person. Denzinger and Schonmetzer, *Enchiridion*, 154, 284, 451.

ing of human nature as a unified whole, not a composite of an "inferior" material part (the body) and a "superior" spiritual part (the soul).

The doctrine of the Trinity is sadly underdeveloped. There are a number of reasons for this. First, the formulation of the doctrine in the first four centuries of the Christian era was in terms of Greek metaphysical concepts, and gave only the bare bones of the doctrine without the inner reality, the marrow. Second, there has been excessive reliance on the genius of people like St. Augustine and St. Thomas Aquinas and, more generally, on the work of celibate theologians. Third, there has been failure on the part of Christians to realize that the Old Testament and the New Testament are intimately interrelated, as the revelation of one and the same eternally triune God. Thus, without Jesus we could never have known of the *fact* of the Trinity; it is to the Old Testament that we must turn for information about the *meaning* of the Trinity.

Trinitarian theory must begin with the words attributed to God by the priestly writer in Genesis:

> God said, "Let us make man in our own image, in the likeness of ourselves" . . .
> God created man in the image of himself,
> in the image of God he created him,
> male and female he created them.
> (Gen 1:26, 27)

St. Justin Martyr and St. Irenaeus interpreted the plural pronouns "us" and "our" in verse 26 as references to the Trinity. Modern scholars of Scripture tend to be more interested in what the priestly author can have meant by these plural forms. Are they honorific, like the royal "we"? Do we have here a trace of primitive polytheism? But I find these questions rather uninteresting. What interests me as a Christian and a trinitarian is that it is the eternally triune God who is at work here. The image of the Trinity is to be found in man as male and female.

We see at once how appropriate this is, and how the celibate theologians have lost sight of the fact. St. Augustine and St. Thomas Aquinas found the image of the Trinity in man's memory, understanding, and will. The single human person seemed to them to be the best image of the thrice-personal God. Thus, a modern Thomist, the late Bernard Lonergan, SJ, could see in the Trinity the perfect community, three persons thinking

Appendix D

with the same intellect, loving with the same will.[3] However, the Trinity is not just a community. It is a community structured as regards origin: it is therefore a family.

We note here the aptness of the words attributed to the first man in Genesis 2:23: "This at last is bone from my bones, and flesh from my flesh!"

This phraseology is curiously echoed in the Nicene Creed: "God from God, light from light, true God from true God" (See, too, Luke 24:39).[4]

Note, too, that the complete image of the Trinity is not in the family as we know it, in which neither parent originates from the other, but in the mythological family described in Genesis, in which the second person ("Eve," "Woman") arises from the first person ("Adam," "Man") and they then become partners and co-principles of a third person in the act of love.

There are imperfections in the analogy, because Eve does not proceed from Adam by knowledge or mental conception, but simply by physical creation. Eve is not begotten of Adam as the eternal Son of God is begotten of the Father before all ages. Here the insights of St. Augustine and St. Thomas Aquinas are necessary and essential. But these insights are incomplete if considered in isolation.

It is necessary to look more deeply into the divine processions as mirrored in creation, and to realize that the Trinity results from an asexual generation leading to a hypersexual act of love. To complete the theory, I must add that this act of love is hermaphroditic and incestuous. I shall explain these terms as I proceed.

Asexual generation exists among the more primitive forms of life. The amoeba reproduces by simple fission, splitting into two amoebas. The paramecium also divides, one paramecium becomes two paramecia.[5] These organisms are simple enough to imitate very closely, on the physical plane, the fecundity of the divine nature. God the Father generates a Son without splitting into parts, simply communicating his identical

---

3. Lonergan, *De Deo trino*, vol. 2, 3rd ed. For a "social" theory of the Trinity, which avoids modern modalism, see Moltmann, *Trinity*.

4. The point is that Luke 24:39 implies that flesh and bones are the very stuff of which humanity is made. Note also the phrase "two in one flesh."

5. The life cycle of the paramecium is described in elementary textbooks of zoology. It is also illustrated in the Natural History Museum, London.

Toward a Modern Theory of the Holy Trinity

nature to a second person. Only the person, as person, is the term of the generative act. No new nature is produced.

The mutual love of Father and Son is a hypersexual act. God is not divided into a male and female principle in the way that some material creatures are divided. God combines in perfect simplicity male strength and female beauty.[6] That is why I have called the divine act of love hermaphroditic. But there is a twin principle of the procession of the Holy Spirit. Therefore I call this act of love hypersexual, which can be taken to mean sexual in a superior, analogous kind of way. (The superiority consists in the fact that both the Father and the Son enjoy the complete and perfect divine nature.)

The act is further incestuous. The Son originates from the Father: Father and Son love each other in the Holy Spirit. (The masculine titles "Father" and "Son" are of course historically conditioned and are not adequate to describe the divine persons. Replacing them by more meaningful titles could be an immense task for feminist theology, or it might be simply impossible).[7]

The prohibition of incest in human society has a biological basis. Endogamy leads to degeneracy. In the family as we know it there is also a psychological reason for this prohibition, based on the biological reason. The love of brother and sister can find no useful sexual expression, and must therefore be kept sacred lest the all-important sexual instinct should be profaned and degraded. I wish to emphasize for the benefit of any puritans who are still with us that it is not the love that is too sacred to be profaned by sex. It is sex that is too sacred to be profaned by such unproductive love.

Many of those who believe in the historical existence of Adam and Eve have been accustomed to say that, in their view of things, man was created with a perfect physical nature. As a result, sexual intercourse between brothers and sisters would not produce degenerate offspring, and this was the means ordained by Providence for the initial propagation of the human race. Of course, I mention this traditional opinion simply for purposes of illustration, and not because I consider it to be historically and theologically tenable.[8]

---

6. In this modern world one must of course add "also female strength and male beauty."

7. Boff, *Trinity*, 120–22, on feminine aspects of the deity.

8. In fact, St. Thomas Aquinas used the example of Adam, Eve, and Abel to illustrate

Appendix D

Now the divine nature is absolutely perfect. It suffers no diminution or loss in being communicated to the Son and to the Holy Spirit. The idea of incest has become distasteful to us for the psychological reasons that I have mentioned. But the prohibition of incest rests on a biological basis. We must purify our consciousness of the primitive taboo and look at the matter in a scientific way if we are to apply the notion of incest to the deity. But I believe that the notion must be applied as an emphatic assertion of the divine fecundity and perfection. The sacred intimacy of that divine act of love combines all that is noblest in the love of brother for sister, husband for wife, father for son, mother for child.[9] We can never grasp its intrinsic perfection and delight. For that reason I hope that this theory will not be misconstrued by the prurient and that it will not prove "offensive to pious ears."

There is a remarkable connection between this theory and a statement made by Freud, after Goethe, in another context. The concluding sentence of Freud's *Totem and Taboo* is this:

In the beginning was the deed.[10]

In this work Freud was expounding his theory that the incest taboo was the basis of the sense of moral obligation. I want to lift this sentence from its context, which is not altogether unrelated to the subject under discussion, and say:

In the beginning was the Deed.

This is, I think, a more comprehensive statement of the doctrine of the Trinity than the opening sentence of the Johannine Prologue:

In the beginning was the Word.

I wish to indicate one or two consequences of this theory.

The highest imitation of the divine life is, I think, the act of sexual reproduction. This is the only action that results in a person. You can think forever, but you will have nothing to show for it except ideas. Sexual

---

the procession of the Holy Spirit from the Father through the Son. *Summa* 1, 36, 3, ad 1.

9. Isaiah 49:15: "Does a woman forget her baby at the breast, fail to cherish the son of her womb? Yet even if these forget, I will never forget you."

10. The original German of this famous sentence is "*Im Anfang war die Tat.*" Freud, *Totem und Tabu*, in *Gesammelte Werke*, vol. 9 (1940) 205 (my translation); Goethe, *Faust*, Part One, 36 (Scene 3, line 1237).

reproduction results in a human person. (Education is clearly needed as well, but it is secondary.) Therefore, I say, it most closely resembles the divine life.

Human sexual activity is not, or ought not to be, a purely biological activity. It is a combination of the biological and the psychological, and has its roots in the depths of the unconscious mind, as Freud discovered. It is, I consider, the highest imitation of the life of the Trinity. The sexual act partakes of the timeless "now" of God's life in a unique way. There is a famous and much parodied reference to this aspect of sex in Ernest Hemingway's novel, "For Whom the Bell Tolls." It is a point that is not usually appreciated. We too readily assume that sexual attraction is a bad joke that nature has played on us because the reproduction of a highly developed organism like ours is a complicated and often difficult process. But I do not think that this assumption expresses the whole story.

My contention that sexual activity is the highest imitation of the life of the Trinity must be seen in perspective, against the background of time and eternity. Sex has its "now," but it is a fleeting instant. In the final state of mankind, it seems that sexual activity will have ceased (cf. Luke 20:36). There will remain psychological activity, when we shall see the Father, Son, and Holy Spirit in a way in which we cannot see them now.

I am not of those who consider that the absence of a sex life is a sign of abnormality. Freud himself allowed for the possibility that the physical side of sex can be sublimated. There are people who find fulfillment in intellectual or artistic pursuits. There are others who renounce a normal sex life in order to serve the common good of society. Christ issued a challenge to celibacy (or so it would seem) for the benefit of "the kingdom of heaven," a phrase that occurs in Matthew's Gospel to designate the kingdom or reign of God that Jesus initiated. Such celibacy, freely undertaken and freely maintained, can be understood as the sacrifice of the greatest personal good to serve the common good of society.

In conclusion, I note that it was no accident that St. Augustine, who had some sexual experience, penetrated so deeply into the mystery of the Trinity; or that St. Thomas, the virginal monk, should have relied so heavily on St. Augustine in developing the doctrine. Nor is it surprising that a married theologian like the late Dr. Frank Sheed could be so much more illuminating on the Trinity than many celibate theologians. Whatever the value of celibacy for the priestly ministry, it seems that its value for dogmatic theology is strictly limited.

Bibliography

Aquinas, Thomas. *Summa Theologiae*. London: Eyre and Spotiswoode, 1963.
———. *Summa Theologica*. Translated by Fathers of the English Dominican Province. London: Burns and Oates, 1947.
Aristotle. *Categories and De Interpretatione*. Translated by J. L. Ackrill. Oxford: Clarendon Press, 1963.
———. *The Metaphysics*. Translated by Hugh Lawson-Tancred. London: Penguin, 1998.
Barth, Karl. *Church Dogmatics* I/2. Translated by G. T. Thompson and H. Knight. Edinburgh: T. & T. Clark, l963.
———. *The Humanity of God*. London: Collins, 1967.
Bauckham, Richard. *Jesus and the Eyewitnesses: The Gospels as Eyewitness Testimony*. Grand Rapids, MI: Eerdmans, 2006.
Beatty, R. A. *Parthenogenesis and Polyploidy in Mammalian Development*. Cambridge: Cambridge University Press, 1957.
Bell, E. T. *Men of Mathematics*. Vol. 2. London: Penguin, 1953.
Boff, Leonardo. *Trinity and Society*. London: Burns and Oates, 1988.
Bond, Helen K. *The Historical Jesus*. London: T. & T. Clark, 2012.
Bonhoeffer, Dietrich. *Letters and Papers from Prison*. Edited by Eberhard Bethge. London: Collins, 1968.
Bouëssé, H., and J.-J. Latour. *Problèmes actuels de christologie*. Paris: Desclée, 1965.
Brower, Reuben A. *On Translation*. New York: Oxford University Press, 1966.
Brown R. E., J. A. Fitzmyer, and R. E. Murphy (eds.). *The Jerome Biblical Commentary*. London: Geoffrey Chapman, 1968.
——— *The New Jerome Biblical Commentary*. London: Geoffrey Chapman, 1997.
Brown, Raymond E. *The Birth of the Messiah*. London: Geoffrey Chapman, 1977.
———. *The Death of the Messiah*. New Haven and London: Yale University Press, 2008.
———. *An Introduction to New Testament Christology*. London: Geoffrey Chapman, 1994.
———. *Jesus God and Man*. London: Geoffrey Chapman, 1968.
Bultmann, Rudolf. *Jesus Christ and Mythology*. London: SCM, 1966.
———. *Theology of the New Testament*. Vols. 1, 2. Translated by Kendrick Grobel. London: SCM, 1968.
Butler, B. C. *The Originality of St. Matthew*. Cambridge: Cambridge University Press, 1951.
———. *Why Christ*. London: Darton, Longman and Todd, 1960.
Byrne, Brendan, S. J. "The Letter to the Philippians." In *NJBC* 48.
Castle, Robert W., Jr. "Litany from the Underground," 1, 2. *The Underground Church*. Edited by Malcolm Boyd. London: Sheed and Ward, 1969.
Christian Renewal. 6 (Summer 1972).

Bibliography

Clarke, Thomas E. "The Humanity of Jesus." *Commonweal* 87, no. 8. November 24, 1967. *Jesus Commonweal papers*, 2.

Cullmann, Oscar. *The Christology of the New Testament*. Translated by Shirley C. Guthrie and Charles A. M. Hall. London: SCM, 1963.

Currer-Briggs, Noel. *Shroud Mafia: The Creation of a Relic?* Lewes: The Book Guild, 1995.

Darwin, Charles. *The Descent of Man, and Selection in Relation to Sex*. Princeton: Princeton University Press, 1981.

Davis, Charles. *The Study of Theology*. London: Sheed and Ward, 1965.

del Colle, Ralph. *Christ and the Spirit: Spirit Christology in Trinitarian Perspective*. New York: Oxford University Press, 1994.

Denzinger, H., and A. Schonmetzer. *Enchiridion Symbolorum, definitionum et declarationum* 34th ed., Freiburg im Breisgau: Herder, 1967.

Dostoyevsky, Fyodor. *Crime and Punishment*. London: Penguin, 1991.

Dunn, James D. G. *Christology in the Making: A New Testament Enquiry into the Origins of the Doctrine of the Incarnation*. 2nd ed. London: SCM, 1989.

Duquoc, Ch. *Christologie. Essai dogmatique. L'homme Jesus*. Paris: Les Editions du Cerf, 1968.

Fenton, J. C. *Saint Matthew*. London: Penguin, 1963.

Fiorenza, Elisabeth Schussler. *In Memory of Her. A Feminist Theological Reconstruction of Christian Origins*. London: SCM, 1983.

———. *Jesus: Miriam's Child, Sophia's Prophet: Critical Issues in Feminist Christology*. London: SCM, 1995.

Fitzmyer, Joseph A., SJ. "The Letter to the Romans." In *NJBC* 51.

Fraenkel, Abraham A. *Abstract Set Theory*. Amsterdam: North-Holland Publishing, 1961.

Freud, Sigmund. *Totem und Tabu*. In *Gesammelte Werke*. Vol. 9 (1940).

Galot, J. *La Personne du Christ*. Brussels: Duculot-Lethielleux, 1969.

Goethe, Johann Wolfgang von. *Faust.Der Tragödie Erster Teil*. Stuttgart: Philipp Reclam, June, 1986.

Goulder, Michael. *Incarnation and Myth: The Debate Continued*. London: SCM, 1979.

———. "Paradox and Mystification" in the above work.

Gribomont, Jean, and André Thibaut. *Richesses et Deficiences des Anciens Psautiers Latins*. In *Collectanea Biblica Latina*. Vol. 13. Rome: Libreria Vaticana, 1959.

Harrington, Daniel J., SJ. *Meeting St. Luke Today*. Chicago: Loyola Press, 2009.

Hawkins, D. B. J. *Being and Becoming*. London: Sheed and Ward, 1954.

Hebblethwaite, Brian. "Incarnation and Atonement: The Moral and Religious Value of the Incarnation." In Goulder, q.v.

Hick, John. *The Metaphor of God Incarnate*. London: SCM, 1993.

———. *The Myth of God Incarnate*, 2nd ed. London: SCM, 1993.

The Hours of the Divine Office in English and Latin. Collegeville, MN: The Liturgical Press, 1964.

Irenaeus. *Adversus Haereses*. In Migne, q.v.

Jung, C. G. *Answer to Job*. Translated by. R. P. C. Hull. London: Routledge and Kegan Paul, 1963.

Kant, Immanuel. *Critique of Pure Reason*. Translated by Norman Kemp Smith. London: Macmillan, 1929.

Karris, Robert J., OFM. "The Gospel According to Luke." In *NJBC* 43.

Kasper, Walter. *Jesus the Christ*. Translated by V. Green. London: Burns and Oates, 1993.

Kittel, G. (ed.). *Theological Dictionary of the New Testament*. Grand Rapids, MI: Eerdmans, 1967.

Bibliography

Knox, Ronald. *The Bible in English*. London: Burns Oates and Washbourne, 1949.
———. *The New Testament in English*. London: Burns Oates and Washbourne, 1947.
———. "The Perfect Flowering of a Human Life." *Tablet* (June 30, 1956), q.v.
Knox, Ronald, and Ronald Cox. *The Gospel Story*. London: Burns and Oates, 1967.
Laubach, Frank. *Did Mary Tell Jesus Her Secret?* London: Marshall, Morgan and Scott, 1970.
Lonergan, Bernard, SJ. *De Deo trino*. Vol. 2, 3rd ed. Rome: Gregorian University Press, 1964.
Lüdemann, Gerd. *The Great Deception: And What Jesus Really Said and Did*. Translated by John Bowden. London: SCM, 1998.
Macquarrie, John. *Jesus Christ in Modern Thought*. London: SCM, 1990.
Maly, Eugene H. "Genesis." In *JBC* 2.
Maritain, Jacques. *The Degrees of Knowledge*. Translated by Gerald B. Phelan. London: Geoffrey Bles, 1959.
Marsh, John. *Saint John*. London: Penguin, 1968.
Marshall, Alfred. *The Interlinear KJV-NIV Parallel New Testament in Greek and English*. Grand Rapids, MI: Zondervan, 1975.
Mascall, E. L. *Existence and Analogy*. London: Darton, Longman and Todd, 1966.
———. *Theology and the Gospel of Christ*. London: SPCK, 1977.
McEleney, Neil J., CSP. "1–2 Maccabees." In *NJBC* 26:73.
McIntyre, John. *The Shape of Christology*. 2nd ed. Edinburgh: T. & T. Clark, 1998.
McKenzie, John L., SJ. "Aspects of Old Testament Thought." In *NJBC* 77.
Meier, John P. *A Marginal Jew: Rethinking the Historical Jesus*. 2 vols. New York: Doubleday, 1991, 1994.
Migne, J. P. *Patrologiae cursus completus, series graeca*. 1857–66.
Mirsky, L. *An Introduction to Linear Algebra*. Oxford: Clarendon Press, 1961.
Missale Romanum. New York: Benziger, 1945.
Moltmann, Jurgen. *The Trinity and the Kingdom of God*. Translated by Margaret Kohl. London: SCM, 1981.
Morris, Thomas V. *The Logic of God Incarnate*. Eugene, OR: Wipf and Stock, 2001.
Moule, C. F. D. *The Origin of Christology*. Cambridge: University Press, 1977, 1999.
Mount Carmel. Vol. 2, no. 3. Winter, 1954.
Murphy, Ronald E. O. Carm. "Psalms." In *JBC* 35:98.
Nédoncelle, M. "Le moi du Christ et le moi des hommes à la lumière de la réciprocité des consciences." In *Problèmes Actuels de Christologie*, q.v.
New Blackfriars. Oxford: Blackfriars, September 1971.
A New Catechism. Introduced by the Bishops of the Netherlands. London: Burns and Oates, 1967.
Nineham, D. E. *Saint Mark*. London: Penguin, 1963.
O'Collins, Gerald, SJ. *Christology: A Biblical, Historical, and Systematic Study of Jesus*. 2nd ed. Oxford: University Press, 2009.
O'Hara, F. "A study of the doctrine of the divinity of Jesus Christ in contemporary thought." PhD diss., University of London, 1971.
O'Hara, Frank. "Incarnation as Translation." *New Blackfriars* 52/616 (September 1971), 417–22.
Pannenberg, Wolfhart. *Jesus—God and Man*. Translated by Lewis L. Wilkins and Duane A. Priebe. London: SCM, 1968.
Patterson, E. M. *Topology*. Edinburgh: Oliver and Boyd, 1963.

Bibliography

Pittenger, W. Norman. *Christology Reconsidered*. London: SCM, 1970.
Poincaré, Henri. "Mathematical Creation." *Mathematics and the Modern World*. San Francisco: W. H. Freeman, 1968.
Quine, Willard V. "Meaning and Translation." *On Translation*. (See under Brower.)
Rahner, K. *Theological Investigations*, 29 vols. London: Darton, Longman and Todd, 1961–92.
Rahner, Karl, and Herbert Vorgrimler. *Concise Theological Dictionary*. London: Burns and Oates, 1965.
Reban, John. *Inquest on Jesus Christ*. Translated by Willi Frischauer. London: Leslie Frewin, l967.
Renan, Ernest. *The Life of Jesus*. Translated by C. E.Wilbour. London: Dent, 1951.
Revue Biblique 31 (1922).
Richardson, Alan (ed.). *A Theological Word Book of the Bible*. London: SCM, 1956.
Richardson, Neil. *John for Today: Reading the Fourth Gospel*. London: SCM, 2010.
Rinaldi, Peter M. *The Man in the Shroud*. London: Sidgwick and Jackson, 1974.
Robinson, John A. T. *Exploration into God*. London: SCM, 1967.
———. *The Human Face of God*. London: SCM, 1973.
Russell, Bertrand. *Why I am not a Christian*. London: Allen and Unwin, 1957.
Schillebeeckx, E. *Christ the Sacrament of Encounter with God*. London: Sheed and Ward, l963.
Schleiermacher, Fredrich. *The Christian Faith*. Edinburgh: T&T Clark, 1976.
Schonfield, Hugh J. *The Passover Plot*. London: Corgi, 1967.
Senior, Donald, CP. "The Miracles of Jesus." In *NJBC* 81: 89–117.
Spurway, H. "Virgin Births." *Lancet* (1955, 2) 967–68 and *NewStatesman and Nation* (Nov. 19, 1955).
The Sunday Missal. London: Collins, 1975.
Tablet. London (Sept. 22, 1951, and June 30, 1956).
Teilhard de Chardin, P. *The Phenomenon of Man*. Translated by Bernard Wall. London: Collins, 1959.
———. *Science and Christ*. Translated by René Hague. London: Collins, 1965.
Temple, William. *Christus Veritas*. London: Macmillan, 1939.
Thibaut, André. See Gribomont.
Tickell, Jerrard. *Odette*. London: Pan Books, 1955.
Tillich, Paul. *The Courage to Be*. London: Collins, 1967.
Vermes, Geza. *The Gospel of Jesus the Jew*. University of Newcastle upon Tyne, 1981.
———. *Jesus the Jew: A Historian's Reading of the Gospels*. 2nd ed. London: SCM, 1994.
Vorgrimler, Herbert. See Rahner.
Wessels, Cletus. *The Mother of God. Her Physical Maternity: A Reappraisal*. River Forest, IL: Aquinas Library, 1964.
Willemse, Johannes. "God's First and Last Word: Jesus." *Concilium*. Vol. 10, no. 1 (December 1965).
Willis, David. "Did He Die on the Cross?" Ampleforth Journal, Spring 1969.
Wilson, Ian. *The Blood and the Shroud*. London: Weidenfeld and Nicoloson, 1998.
———. *The Shroud: Fresh Light on the 2000-year-old Mystery*. London: Bantam, 2010.
Winter, Michael. *The Atonement*. London: Geoffrey Chapman, 1995.
Young, Frances. "Incarnation and Atonement: God Suffered and Died." In *Incarnation and Myth: The Debate Continued*, edited by Michael Goulder, 101–3. London: SCM, 1979.

www.ingramcontent.com/pod-product-compliance
Lightning Source LLC
Chambersburg PA
CBHW070943160426
43193CB00011B/1795